How to be

Kinkier

More Adventures in Adult Playtime

Morpheous

Green Candy Press

How to Be Kinkier
ISBN 978-1-931160-94-0
Published by Green Candy Press
www.greencandypress.com

Printed in Canada by Transcontinental
Massively Distributed by P.G.W.

Dedication

Mary, Elle and Effi—Thank you for all your wonderful support over the years.

Contents

Introduction

I became aware of Morpheous a few years back when he sent me a copy of his excellent first book for beginner kinksters, *How to Be Kinky*. I was struck right away by its honesty, accessibility, practicality, inclusivity, good humor and confident, friendly tone, which clearly arose from his lived experience as a happy kinkster. I recognized him instantly as a fellow traveler, someone dedicated to unlocking the mysteries, power, beauty and grace of sexuality by using his erotic nature as his guide. We each became comfortable in our skin, not just to have a rocking good time in bed, but also to share that deep understanding with others in a physical way, body to body. We've turned the adage, "Those who can't do, teach," on its head. We teach *because* we can "do," the public teaching stemming from the private doing, as naturally as breathing.

Whatever else it may be, sex is, at its heart, a physical practice and dance, akin to martial arts, a tea ceremony, yoga or ballet. Becoming an effective sex partner requires a lot of practice and focus and that goes triple for kinky sex. Morpheous has done the heavy lifting for you regarding the practical aspects of kinky play, including how to think about adding kink to your sex life, and he has laid this information out for you in both his books. This enables interested parties to more effectively negotiate satisfactory relationships, be they for a night or a lifetime.

In the first book Morpheous spent a lot of time explaining the basics, such as "what is a whip?" "How does one use it?" "Why would one want to whip or be whipped?" "How can I safely tie up my partner?" and "What are good body postures to help get me/my partner in the proper mood?"; in short, all of the information one would need to transition from having regular, "vanilla" sex to creating a scenario precisely designed to drive the participants crazy with desire, and then satisfying

Facing Page: Keep your sub under control at all times!

that desire in ways never before imagined. For that conversation, *How to Be Kinky* is a most excellent primer.

As the late-night TV ads say, "But wait, there's more!" That "more" is the topic of this book. How does a couple that wants to invite a third party into the bedroom or playspace do so? What questions should we ask, both of ourselves as well as our potential partner? Of what must we be aware before we even attempt making real such a common fantasy? Morpheous makes it clear how best to proceed. Moving beyond the occasional, casual threesome, the author also delves deeply into the issues that arise when two people in a committed relationship decide that they'd like to explore polyamory. He offers good, practical guidelines for that conversation as well as an overview of the potential pitfalls.

What if a couple decides that it wants to expand the roles that the members inhabit during play outside the bedroom and into more of daily life (so-called "24/7" couples)? There's a LOT to know before deciding to make your entire life a form of contemplative foreplay and erotic devotion and Morpheous brings his considerable experience to bear on this timely subject. He knows that in situations like this there is no one-size-fits-all answer, only the solutions relevant to the couple in question. Kinky sex, like all sexual relations, is expressly "built to suit."

What about advanced toys such as electrical gizmos and the like? Morpheous helps the reader past their concerns and tells us how to use them both effectively as well as safely. He does the same with advanced bondage techniques, moving beyond the simple, four-point restraint on a comfy bed to more complicated setups using other furniture. No matter how far out the scenarios may be, Morpheous never loses sight of the first imperative of kinky sex: safety first. Since he wants us all to live to play another day he devotes an entire chapter on safety issues, from the "Duh, of course!" moment to points a more novice player would never imagine.

As with any other affinity group, kinky people are part of a community, with community standards, meetings, get-togethers (in kinky speak, "munches"), conventions (local, state, regional and national), pagents, websites, workshops, books and the like, the better for like-minded people to be able to find each other, be it for business, pleasure or mating purposes. Morpheous tells it like it is about how to become a member in good standing of one's local kink organization, and how best to participate in it, be it as a host of a munch or play party, or the leader of it. Except for the behavior of the members, it's not a lot different from the Rotary club, believe it or not—and what they do behind closed doors might be more similar than we imagine!

For those who want to professionalize their kink, either in front of the camera or behind it, the author does an excellent job of laying out, exactly, what it means to be a professional model or a kink photographer. What's expected of each person in that role? How can one advance from being strictly amateur to actually getting paid for what has been, so far, just done for fun? How does one keep oneself safe, or create a workplace that is safe? If you think you may want to go down that path, this book is worth the price of admission just for that chapter alone.

Very few people take their first foray into kink and don't find themselves wanting more; this book, then, is the entrée to *How To Be Kinky*'s appetizer. It will satiate your hunger for a more fulfilling and thrilling kink encounter, and it will pave your way into a full-time kinky lifestyle, if that's what you're looking for. Either way, I'm sure that by the time you've finished, you'll be hungry for dessert!

Nina Hartley
Los Angeles
September, 2011

Chapter One

What is Kinkier?

It is not enough to conquer; one must learn to seduce.
—Voltaire

Oftentimes couples and singles that have spent time exploring a variety of kinks and found them to be enjoyable will want to branch out into exploring new territory, but before taking that next step several questions might ask themselves: how do you know if you are ready to take your kinky play to the next level? What might the next level actually be? Is advanced sex bondage for you, or perhaps medical scenes that involve pretty shiny things that go "into" people? Does being "kinkier" mean you create a more extensive wardrobe or toy box or just become more creative with what you have? Should you own a slave or give yourself completely to a Mistress or Master? How can you know when the time is right, and that everything will be all right afterward? Is it kinkier to handcuff your boyfriend in a bathroom stall of the Hard Rock Café in Vegas while you blow him or is it kinkier to spend six hundred dollars on a new leather outfit that hugs your body like a second skin and makes you feel like the personification of sex in high heels? What about using nipple clamps that have been kept in the freezer, or fitting a butt plug inside your lover and then tying it in place and making her get dressed so you can take her to dinner at an expensive restaurant with it lodged secretly in place? How about leaving naughty voice mails for your lover describing in detail the filthiest things you can imagine and how you are going to do them to her when she gets home, knowing full well that

Facing Page: Is there any combination more exciting than a paddle and a bare ass?

How to Be Kinkier

Getting kinkier is all about finding your deepest desires and exploring them for real.

when she picks up that message she is in a business meeting and just the sound of your voice makes her nipples stiffen every so slightly under her silk blouse, which you hope the others around her will notice? What about dressing up in your sexiest outfit and meeting your lover at a bar, pretending you don't know each other, and then picking each other up and renting a sleazy motel room and fucking like animals? Would it be even kinkier if you paid your wife afterward like a slutty whore, or did things to her that were outside your regular sex life, like cumming on her face and telling her she is a tramp? What about buying 70 feet of plaster wrap at a medical supply store and casting your submissive on a Friday night and then fucking him while he is immobilized in the exact position you desire?

What does it mean to be kinkier and how is that different from regular kink? In this book I am going to explore some of the ways that you can intensify your sex life, from extra toys to simple and complex scenarios. We love toys in the kink world, from exquisite floggers to amazingly devious ball gags, but keep in mind that it isn't always just about the equipment; making things kinkier is also about taking existing ideas or situations and twisting them to achieve a new outcome from even a

You're only limited by your imagination—or the filthiest ideas of your Top!

Women with a new manicure or long nails: some lip balm packed under your nail will help stop you from scratching your clit when you masturbate.

familiar object or sensation. It all starts in the head: how twisted and devious is *your* mind? How twisted can it be? Pretty twisted, I'm betting. I'm sure you'll have more than a few tasty ideas in mind before you even pick up this book.

In exploring your kinkier side—taking your interests and ramping them up—will you be putting your own or someone else's safety or health at risk, physically or emotionally, just to get your rocks off? Where is your personal limit and what does that mean for your partner's safety? How do you negotiate these issues so that everyone plays safely while still retaining the heated passion of kinkier playtime? When you play at a higher level of intensity, it's all the more vital that you know you will be safe and that your partner will feel safe as well.

Getting kinkier is all about your own personal journey. Take as much time as you need to explore all the subtle nuances in your sex life in a healthy, positive way. While there are many people who can mentor you in various activities or protocols when you are making your life kinkier, the best judge of your evolution is you. If you make conscious decisions that are positive and encouraging for yourself and for your partners, you should have a very good idea of where you are and where you want to go while exploring kinkier sex. Mentors can help provide perspective for your journey but ultimately the journey is not theirs. However you want to be, you should own those feelings and desires. Knowing yourself is the best way for you to judge when to ebb and when to flow with your experiences. There will always be times when you want to try something new and the whole situation goes sideways. When we play at a higher level, we want to play with partners that know us, understand us, and will help support us. The true mark of someone's character isn't revealed during the soft fluffy moments in our lives when everything is going great, but rather during times of challenge. Playing with activities that are higher risk requires you to be much more cognizant of what is going on, whether you are a bottom, a Top, a slave or a Mistress. You should always be willing to be accountable for your actions or activities, and be able to step out of a role and be a responsible and caring person to your partner if things go awry.

Facing Page: Shelling out on a perfectly-fitting latex body suit can be the next step into kink.

Riding crops come with a lot of different and fun tips.

Honing Your Desire

What you want deep down and what you may think you want can be disconnected. I have seen this happen many times, especially with people who have some experience at kinky sex under their belts (or bedsheets!) but who are still learning about how to take things to another level. Perhaps there is something you want to explore—a particular activity or situation—but then when you actually have the experience, it doesn't deliver the satisfaction you had anticipated. This is normal when you are exploring the myriad of possibilities with kinkier sex. It happens. Helping your partner talk about what he or she wants and listening closely will help both of you in the future for kinky exploration. Trying to figure out what the nugget of your interest is can take time, but the exploration can be fun!

For example: A submissive of mine once expressed the desire to be to be tied down very tightly and have an elaborate ritual performed on her. After that, she wanted to be penetrated, repeatedly, and called dirty, filthy, nasty names, the kind of names that would not only make her mother blush but would damn her entire family to the seventh level of hell. But

Boot licking is a very powerful emotive experience for slaves.

during our playdate I found that the specific act of tying her up wasn't elic-
iting the response she was hoping for. The bondage she requested wasn't
fitting in with the overall flow of the scene; it felt contrived and pushed.
The scene was missing a certain intensity and passion and her actions were
contradicting what she said she desired when it came to bondage specifically. Her body language showed that she wasn't reacting to the bondage
the way I had anticipated; she wasn't particularly squirmy, nor was she
dropping into a nice headspace. In her eyes there was a disconnectedness,
something lacking: that spark of passion when you both are intensely into
the scene and connected with each other. We tried to pick it up on the fly
as we played and the overall scene was enjoyable but not as much fun as
either of us had hoped. Afterward when we were relaxing and lounging
around my loft in various states of undress while we slowly put ourselves
back together, I prodded her gently with pertinent questions such as "How
does it feel when you are bound versus when you are just told to stay still?"
"What types of names do you find the most degrading versus the most
arousing?" "How do those names make you feel and why?" Asking about

Coil your rope
in butterfly coils
to reduce the
tangles and
snags.

7

How to tie pierced nipples with a ribbon

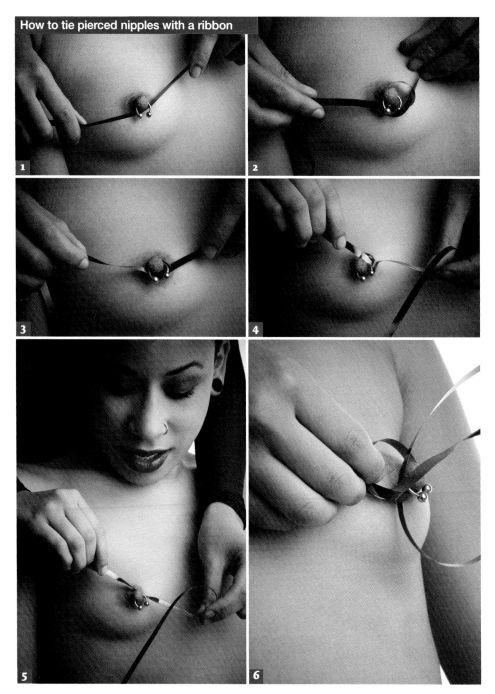

1 Nipple piercings can make nipple play more interesting with a little ribbon. 2 They act as an anchor for your sexy time with their nipples. Tie a regular overhand knot behind the piercing, on top of the nipple. 3 Snug it down but not too tight. You are going for mmmm not ooowwwww! 4 Finish it with a second knot. 5 Mmm, pretty! 6 Do the same to the other nipple; you don't want it to feel left out.

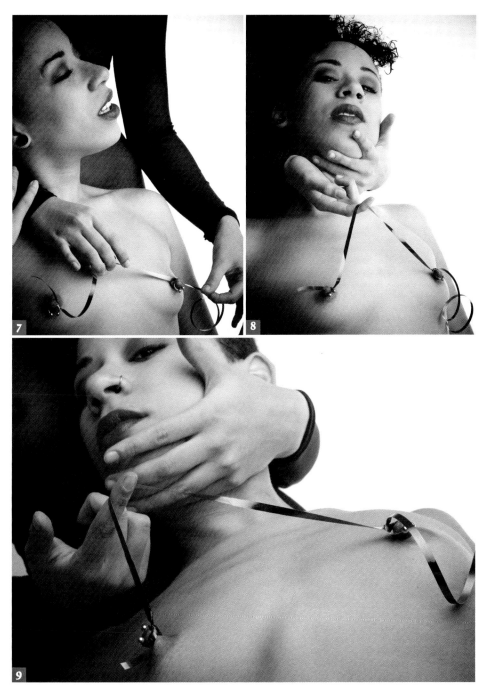

7 And finish it too with a second knot. 8 A firm steady tug will make your submissive follow you anywhere. 9 I said anywhere!

Poor little wet girl...

A woman's scarf or man's necktie is just as strong as quarter-inch nylon rope.

her other fantasies and searching out a common thread in those led me to understand, and she eventually confirmed this the next time we played, that instead of a specific activity such as being bound and immobilized, what she really desired was license to give away her agency in making choices; to find freedom psychologically in the role and bondage, not having to make decisions, rather than just the physical act of being bound, seemed to be the keystone for her play. That was her "nugget." Her desire to be bound and not have to make a decision was interesting and was a point of departure, but she also loved the dirty, filthy things I said to her during a scene, things that would objectify and dehumanize her. She yearned to have her everyday persona driven out of her for an hour or two and to just be instructed to act and perform. She desired humiliation that assailed her for not being sufficiently "trampy," which is a delicious contradiction to her everyday, vanilla life where she normally strove to be a "good girl." She wanted to be called a slut and a whore and forced to act like one in playtime. For her it was not having that "choice" between the two roles and being forced into that role of "trampy girl" that excited her

A gimp mask will make your slave feel like the sexual toy that they are.

If you don't have any rope and if your partner is flexible enough to fold her arms behind her back, you can use a pillowcase to tie her up in a hotel room. Detailed on page 57.

most. It gave her the chance to have some inner quiet and peace while having a break from her real world, to turn down the volume of the noise of everyday life and be in the moment doing something she enjoyed where she could revel in the position of her own chosen submission, rather than the act of being bound.

The need for this sort of fine-tuning can be typical, and for both Dominant and submissive, this journey can be revealing in more ways than one. Finding the right partner to play with, who is supportive and just as kinky as you, will help you explore the subtle nooks and crannies of your sexual interests, and this is going to be a lot more fun than keeping quiet and repressing your desires or acquiescing without speaking up for what is important to you.

Here are some tips for teasing out your desires if you are not sure

1. Ask yourself some clear and blunt questions about what you like and why you like it. Example: does flogging get me hot while I am bound and helpless or do I just like the sensation of flogging?

2. Is there a common element between a particular desire or fantasy you have that crosses into other ones? For example, a damsel in distress fantasy that leaves you hot and wet might be due more to a bondage fetish than a pirate fetish if the bondage continually pops up time and time again regardless of the scenario playing in your fantasies.

3. When something new of interest comes up in your playtime or fantasies, is it the newness that is exciting or the sensations?

4. Do you take some time to process and investigate new sensations before you decide if you like them or not? Example: you might give a single-tail whip a few scenes to explore all of the subtle and not so subtle sensations it delivers, before deciding if you want to keep working with it.

5. How do you feel after you have had a chance to play with these new sensations or toys or fantasies?

6. Does what you are interested in involve you crossing any of your personal values or boundaries, and if so, how are you going to mentally or emotionally manage that?

Facing Page: Have fun with your submissive!

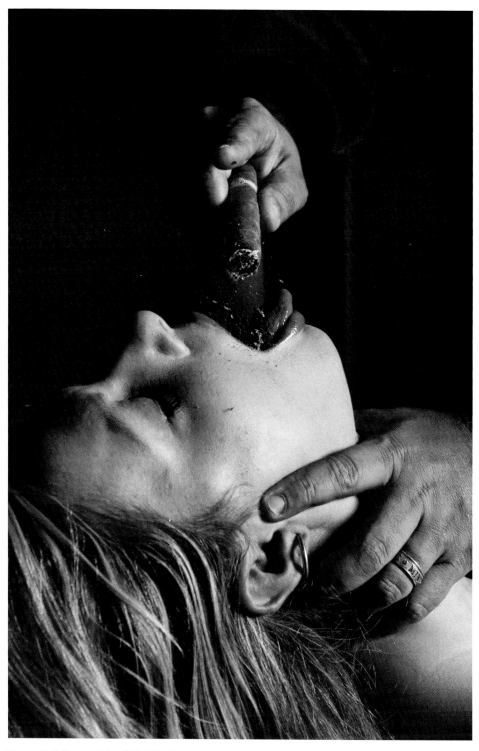

Those that like smoking fetish like it a lot.

All of us who are into kinky play take part for a multitude of reasons. In *How to Be Kinky: A Beginner's Guide to BDSM*, I outlined how you go about finding partners whose interests and aims match your own. In this chapter, I will assume you have found someone you can explore with—someone who is as nonjudgmental toward your kinks as you are to his or hers; someone who is positive and encouraging and supportive in your exploration. When I meet someone new and we are both interested in playing, as a Dominant I find it helpful to ask certain questions that can help me suss out what it is that makes my potential partner tick. This doesn't have to be in interview—just raise questions as you are both getting to know each other that will help you both figure out where a playdate scene has the potential to go, because we all want a scene to be mind-blowing, amazing, hot, sweaty, nasty, filthy and intense, one that leaves both of us disheveled and sticky. Doing a little groundwork beforehand to figure out the sexual landscape for both of you will help it turn into all that! Some of the questions I like to ask may seem quite simple—and they are—but I find that simpler questions can lead to very detailed answers.

Clothespins work well as improvised nipple clamps, but so do chopsticks with elastic bands on the ends!

1. How does it make you feel when you engage in _____ [activity]?
2. How does it make you feel when you are told to _____ ?
3. What do you love the most about doing _____ to/with me or others?
4. What are your two most favorite activities/kinds of play to engage in with a partner?

The answers to these questions can give you a solid idea of where their interests lie and can help you build up to "The Mind Fuck." A solid, hot, nasty and delicious mind fuck will challenge your partner's comfort level. Psychologically it can create a strong emotional response. Depending on how you set it up, it can play with joy, anger, fear or humiliation, and can create other charged responses. A good mind fuck enhances play between two people, rather than detracting. It is not abuse, and because it walks a very fine line, right up to the razor's edge of psychological play, it can have negative effects if you go too hard too fast or take it in a direction your partner is not prepared for.

Advanced players who engage in mind fucking not only know what their boundaries are but more importantly what their partner's are. This is not something you should engage in casually, unless you have developed a

A bootlace is great for on-the-spot CBT.

strong level of trust with your partner. Typically it involves misdirection—taking the scene one way that is not challenging and putting your play partner into a nice headspace and then abruptly changing direction into territory that he or she finds challenging. The situation can be set up long in advance and it should be something the submissive desires to explore but may not have the experience or courage required to explore it on his own. Writing from a Dominant's perspective, when I introduce a mind fuck into my scening activity, I will initially go slowly, so I can judge my partner's response. Long before setting up the mind fuck you should take the time to ask questions and get a solid idea of what will or won't work once you begin. For example, I might ask questions in a nonthreatening environment with my partner when we are not playing, for instance, at dinner:

"When we play, what do you find really pushes your psychological buttons in a good way and a bad way? Are there any emotional or mental landmines that would affect a scene where we would explore kinkier play? What values are important to you and which ones are flexible? How would you feel if I did _____?" This will give you the ingredients to build your masterpiece from; the bottom has to have input into the "ingredients" but not necessarily control over the "recipe." A mind fuck is hot if done right and terrifying or possibly tragic if done wrong. It can be like walking through a psychological minefield and I recommend only doing it if you and your partner know each other very well.

This mind fuck began as my wife and I were getting ready to attend the Montreal Fetish Weekend, an annual party involving hundreds of people. I wanted to transform her from my slave and wife into a rubber latex gimp who was completely dependent on me. I had a whole latex body outfit made for her, complete with a hood that had no holes for eyes or ears, only a mouth hole for breathing and other uses. Removing her sight and most of her sound and forcing her to concentrate on taking my commands and being completely dependent on me put her in a headspace she had never been in before. I sealed her head in the hood and led her on my leash through the hotel lobby, out the door and down the street to the venue. People stared and some asked to take pictures. All night I would say, "Here, watch my slave," and then hand the leash to someone, without her knowing if it was a friend or someone else. I wanted her to feel that she might very well be abandoned as this rubber gimp doll to be objectified by the crowd when in truth I was never more than ten feet away all

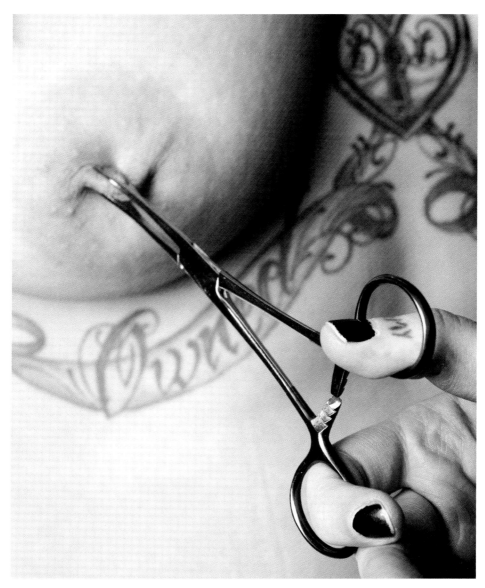

Even simple clamps can be wicked in the right hands.

night long. I had other people grope her; sometimes half a dozen people would be stroking her, pinching, slapping and disorienting her. Without her sight her sense of touch was heightened, and every hand on her body, coupled with the mind fuck of quite possibly being abandoned, of being dismissed as a rubber gimp doll, no longer a person with feelings and emotions, just there for the pleasure of the crowd, was intense and overwhelming.

—Retrodeviant, Master

A dollar store can provide you with enough pervertible toys to get you through two Saturdays and a Sunday on a Friday night.

Here's an example from my own experience. A submissive I know is terrified of slimy, squirmy things; they really creep her out. She is also really interested in fear play and coercion within a scene. Her big fantasy involved having a Dominant take control of her through coercion and "trick" her into performing nasty, lewd acts on another woman—a forced bisexual experience. This was something she would never engage in in her vanilla life. One day I told her that for our next playdate she would indeed be frightened and that she would do exactly as I said or else the scene would be over.

Our playdate came and I started the scene off nice and soft with some sensual bondage, taking the time to tie her gently and get her all nicely secured. All the while I was telling her what a good girl she is, how beautiful and desirable she is until she was all relaxed and her defenses were down. After about an hour of soft, sensual play, I started bringing in the elements of the mind fuck I wanted to bring about. "You know, baby, I have been noticing lately that you have always had an aversion to learning how to go down on women when we play. I think that perhaps it is time you learned your place as my slut, one that will do as I say." This works well if the situation has "one foot in reality," such as a reluctance to suck cock or worship pussy, but is something they do have an interest in and are too shy or reluctant to try. This particular submissive enjoyed forced bi encounters but had a hard time acting on her desires because that "isn't what good girls do." "Slut training" should involve something that is a part of the person's play persona and situation, not something that is randomly grabbed out of the air. I kept the dirty talk up about how much I enjoy seeing her with other women, watching her eat pussy and knowing she "hates" it. Then another Domme arrived right on time (scheduled for later in the afternoon and in on it all). As the doorbell rang I said, "Oh, I almost forgot your surprise!" In walks the Mistress in tall bitch boots and long sweeping leather dress. "You know, my concern that you don't enjoy eating pussy is something that detracts from your service to me and we are going to fix that today." At this point she protests and that she is "never going to eat pussy—never ever!" "Oh, I think you will," I said. She gave me an adamant stare that clearly indicted her "refusal" to eat out my Domme friend. "Right now you get a choice between eating her pussy, or the surprise under this towel," which is where I had the tool stashed that would help me to apply pressure in this situation. She was vehement that she wasn't going to eat pussy, no way, no how, never, and with a smug smile chose what was under the towel. "You are sure about that?" I asked,

Making a few adjustments on a slave 2.0.

and indeed she was. Pulling the pink Hello Kitty towel off the Nalgene bottle filled with one dozen leeches, I watched her eyes widen and I will never forget the look she gave me, her mouth widened into an O.

She seemed to have lost her breath for a moment. After her breath came back to her she immediately started stammering, "Wait, wait, WAIT, WAIT, hang on!" (But she wasn't using her safeword so I knew it would be okay to continue.) She started protesting that this wasn't what she signed up for; I wasn't really going to use them on her, was I? I was pretty happy I had her tied down nice and tight. As she protested and complained and tried to bargain with some other perceived advantage or skill she had (the typical stages are very similar to other situations where people are put in pressure situations: refusal, denial, bargaining and then acceptance if you do it right). I calmly and slooooowly snapped on some rubber gloves (I enjoy adding to

When punching, you can use the heel of your palm to strike if your knuckles get sore.

the dramatic tension by being slow and methodical—it gives the "victim" more time to think and ramps up his or her anxiety). Then I unscrewed the top of the Nalgene bottle that had the squirming and writhing leeches in it, purchased from a bait shop the day before. The nice thing about a curved plastic container is it distorts the size of the leeches so they look about twice as big as they actually are. All the while I was pretending to ignore her "bargaining." Slowly reaching into the jar with a long pair of forceps I put the jar down near her and gently drew out one of the larger, more vigorously squirming leeches and held it over her chest, the occasional drop of leech water falling to her smooth skin and making her shiver and squirm even more. "I'm sorry, were you saying something about not liking pussy? That's a shame, because this bad boy looks hungry…" At this point the wall around her "boundary" began to crack as a strangled sob started deep in her chest and her eyes started tearing, never looking away from the squirming leech held over her chest and only 16 inches from her face. Then I slowly started lowering it toward her breasts and as her sobbing and crying increased I could see how she was giving in and realizing that the only way out of this situation was to give proper tongue service to the Domme sitting comfortably in the chair across the room, watching with an amused grin on her face. I'll give the submissive credit, I had to lower the leech right to within an inch of her tender, supple nipple before she relented with a primal whine and said, "Oh god, please, no, no, no! I'll do anything you want. I'll eat her pussy just like you want, Sir!" I paused for a long, long moment, letting the leech continue to flip and twist around the end of the forceps as I considered her acquiescence, pausing and deliciously reveling in her predicament, and then slowly returning the leech to the jar, I screwed the lid back on and put the jar over beside my Domme friend where it would be in her line of vision when the submissive was between her legs. I then untied her and my Domme friend took over with teaching her how to give proper tongue worship while I watched enjoyably.

This is an elaborate scene I know, and requires time and effort to set up. You don't have to build something as elaborate when you start out. By the way, leeches are "in season" up in more northern climates in bait shops only in the spring and summer. Or you can order them off the Internet year round. As far as proper disposal when I'm done, I go pickerel fishing!

Facing Page: Sharing a vacuum cube can be lots of fun!

Veterinarian wrap is cheap and comfy to use for bondage and it comes in a wide variety of colors.

Girls, don't let men have all the fun—get your own cock!

How to Set Up a Mind Fuck

1. Tell them in advance that you are going to do something special that will push their boundaries the next time you play. Don't tell them what it entails, just that if they are willing, "something special" will happen.

2. Start the scene out in a nice direction they are used to. Get them comfortable and do things they like. Let them think you have forgotten about your "promise."

3. Frame the new departure as a "choice" for them. Make the choice you want them to pick the lesser of the two evils.

4. You HAVE to be willing to follow through with either choice–the punishment, or the reward. If your partner perceives you will not follow through on your "threats," then the scene will fall apart.

5. Create the scene around something that does not contradict their primary boundaries, only boundaries that are somewhat flexible. A mind fuck should ultimately be fun for everyone involved; it is *not* abuse.

Exercise bands are long, stretchy rubber strips used for physiotherapy patients: awesome for bondage!

You can push your own boundaries. We get better by pushing and practice but don't go so far outside your comfort zone that you end up in the deep end of the pool without being prepared for it! Have a solid idea of what is going to happen when you do this particular activity, and if you don't know for sure, then go slow and steady. Slow is safe. Most important of all, whatever your evolution and skill set is, don't use other people's experiences as a standard to measure yourself against. This is your journey and exploration and you are responsible for it.

Five Key Points for Stepping Up the Action:

■ Use your own comfort level as a guide for your sexual adventures.

■ To start, come up with a new use or twist on a sensation you are familiar with.

■ A mind fuck is hot, but it is not abuse.

■ Playing with activities that are higher risk requires you to pay closer attention to what is happening and to be mentally and emotionally present.

■ If you don't know how they're doing—ask. Keeping an open line of communication with your partner is essential.

Chapter Two

Advanced Negotiation

Le couple qui vient au ménage à trois n'est pas toujour celui qui part. (The couple that comes to a threesome isn't always the one that leaves.)
—Anonymous

Sometimes we may get so caught up in the intoxicating newness of our kinky experiences and the resultant relationships that we put aside the tools we need to ensure our own personal emotional safety. This happens with newbies and it also happens with established people in the lifestyle. We're so eager for new experiences that we forget to hang on to our own core values and a basic respect for boundaries, our own and our partners'. Establishing and reestablishing your boundaries requires frequent negotiation with your partners and constant introspection. There are times when it is far braver to say, "I love you but this activity isn't for me," and let your partner go off to satiate that desire with someone else. It requires a level of comfort with yourself that is often difficult to achieve when you are still learning how to be kinkier. There are going to be times when your kink limits or your partner's limits are pushed beyond what you both might be comfortable with. This is a natural evolution in learning to be kinkier and shouldn't be feared; you need to face it, own it and make it work for you.

There are opportunities to taste many experiences when you are taking your kinky life to the next level. It is important to have a support system in place comprised of your partner, friends, or colleagues who will be there for you as you expand your boundaries into previously uncharted territory. These should be people you trust and care about, who care about

Facing Page: Have you been a bad boy?

Be a good slave and lick your mistress' shoes and don't miss a spot.

EMT shears are cheap and you should have more than one pair.

you and your ongoing evolution. You need to surround yourself with people who recognize that you will evolve over time. You may not wind up the same in a few years as when you were a newbie dipping your toe tentatively into the warm waters of the kinky world. If you have a partner who is willing to encourage you to explore your kinky side then you are already ahead of the game. But what if you have a major kink—something intense and toe-curlingly satisfying to you—that you really love but your partner just can't get into? How do you navigate the emotional boundaries of being in a couple and still get what you both want? There are some definite pitfalls associated with negotiating your way through this situation. In addition, there is a problem more experienced people may encounter, something I call "kink fatigue."

Navigating all of this requires skillful negotiation. In *How to Be Kinky* we looked at basic ways of negotiating your desires with the person in your primary relationship, and how to best reach a compromise through acknowledging those boundaries that both (or all) of you are comfortable with. In this chapter I'll offer some directions for finding your way through the tangled forest of human sexuality and more complex issues that will arise now that you are well past the newbie stage, with an emphasis on negotiating your way through it so that you and your partner(s) can be comfortable with how your relationships evolve. Bring your machete and compass—and don't forget the nipple clamps!

It is essential to learn what really works for you, know yourself and your needs and desires, and then be able to communicate that to your partner(s). While always taking pains to play safe, try things that might push your own boundaries from time to time just to see if they are still in the same place as you left them. They might not be, and you will learn something more about yourself in discovering that. Having a strong value system provides you with a scaffold for a M/s (Master/slave) structure, enabling you to build upon your experiences and create a kinky life that is your own unique pastiche. Some use M/s as a model for their daily lives and some let it complement theirs. Involving your partner in the decision-making process to ensure both of you are comfortable with what is happening will make this transition smoother. Regardless of the outcome, positive or negative, you should always conduct yourself with grace and dignity while exploring M/s. Be a person who keeps his word, says what he means and means what he says. This never goes out of style regardless of which lifestyle—Master/slave, Dominant/submissive, Top/bottom—you lead.

Whether or not a relationship is D/s or M/s oriented, it still has within it all the components of what we term a vanilla relationship; including the need for clear communication and skillful negotiation. That is a reality that I and many others engaging in kink relationships fail to grasp when relationships that we truly believe we have negotiated start to flounder and fail. Relationships in general follow a pattern or stages, beginning with infatuation. We become infatuated with the discovery of kink first and with finding venues to express our kink, a stage in which our hormones tend to be the driving force. It still strikes me how little my wife (now my submissive) and I knew about one another after months of dating. In reality, we had discovered certain likes and dislikes in conversations with one another, yet we had not plumbed the psychological depths of our characters. All the long conversations into the wee, small hours of the morning did not uncover how conditioned we were, what emotionally squicked us about the other person, and what psychological landmines might we encounter. It was only as our relationship evolved and we stepped on those landmines that we found how critical it is to have clear, genuine communication and to emotionally risk engaging in negotiations. —Kindred, Sadist/Therapist.

Spreading water-based lube on someone's feet and then letting it dry will make his feet extra ticklish.

Negotiating Styles

The fingernail test is a great quick way to determine if a playmate's circulation is good when you've got them tied up. Squeeze a fingernail firmly and then release. If it goes from white to pink immediately, the person is all right.

We all want to experience what gets us off. Sharing our fantasies and playing them out in the bedroom or dungeon is part of what makes all of kinky sex so risqué! But how do you negotiate with your partner so that it's a win-win situation? What if you have a kink that is not even on the same planet as your partner, or even if it is and you really want her to indulge you, how do you best approach the subject? You might have an urge that is really juicy deep inside you but because it is so close to your ultimate desires, you might be shy about sharing it with someone else. What follows are three basic negotiating types that I see continually surface in the BDSM lifestyle. I cannot claim to have invented these terms; they are gleaned from common knowledge and my experiences over the years. Familiarize yourself with these types so that you can both recognize which style you are dealing with and figure out the best techniques for negotiating with them. Think of it as understanding another language—the more languages you speak, the better you and your partner will be at getting what you both want. These negotiation types are the Aggressive, the Passive and the Ingenious.

The Aggressive negotiator feels that he or she must win in all negotiations. These individuals base their style of negotiation on the concept of "winners and losers" and they certainly will try in every negotiation to be the winner. For them, negotiation is as much a game of power struggle as it is about getting what they want. They may not really care much about the other person's feelings or sometimes even the results as long as they win win win! These are the Dommes that must be in control regardless of the cost. They don't feel comfortable if they don't have their hands on the wheel at all times and will not hesitate to use distraction and chaos to confuse their partners, just to keep them off balance and second guessing their position. They also are not above lying to cover up their inability to master a situation. It is always about their success and the defeat of the other party and it can be difficult to negotiate with partners like this because they fail to see creative opportunities to bring resolution to a situation. Unfortunately these types also tend to fail to learn anything from their mistakes along the way, and don't mind having other people bear the brunt of their learning curve. Be forewarned, this personality can also take the form of someone who is quiet and thoughtful, who has a lot of resources available

Facing Page: Gas masks can be super hot in any scene.

Glass toys are beautiful and lots of fun!

to him. They don't always blow in like a hurricane, they can smile and be subtle but recognizing their style early is key to making sure you get what you need without losing anything you have gained.

How do you recognize an Aggressive negotiator? They will use "I" language constantly in their description of themselves and their abilities "I am the only one that can teach you this, I am the only one who can show you how to serve properly, I am the only one that can introduce you to the community, I am the only one that is qualified to teach proper safety to DMs, et cetera..." Their style is based on egocentricity; they are the center of a universe where you are led to believe that without them, all would be lost.

How do you deal with an Aggressive negotiator? You have to be well prepared and wearing your figurative sparring equipment and chest protector because you are constantly going to need to be on your guard. Offer them alternative choices and refuse to be backed into a corner or bullied into a position. They may try to introduce variables that were never agreed upon. Logic works well in negotiating with this type. List your issues and position,

How to use a long leash to tie up your slave

1 Take an extra long leash. This one is made by Pendragon Chainmail. 2 It happens to come with swivel clasps on both ends. 3 Tina drops the leash down through the D swivel... 4 to make a loop... 5 which she then slips over Kat's wrist. 6 Then she brings the leash around the other wrist...

7 and clips it into place... 8 trapping Kat's wrists and holding her secure. 9 Tina then turns our lovely victim around... 10 and brings her wrists up and over behind her head. 11 Then she wraps it around Kat's waist... 12 and pulls it through.

13 Ooo, now it is getting to the good part! She drops the chain down between her legs... 14 and back up through to the front again. 15 She comes up over the waist band and back down to clip the other end to the crotch chain. 16 Now when Kat struggles she will pull on the crotch chain that is directly over her clit and pussy! 17 Turn her around and give her a smack. You did a great job Tina!

When meeting a prospective online partner in real life, picking a public place for the initial meeting is completely acceptable. Don't let them tell you otherwise.

be polite and calm and if their emotions get heated and demanding, walk away and let their little tempest blow itself out before picking up and trying again. This might take five minutes or five days. Patience is your most valuable ally. Be prepared to walk away, as the Aggressive negotiator is a stubborn one. If you wind up on the high ground with an Aggressive negotiator, be prepared to hear him or her suddenly offer up a trade-off situation. If they perceive they are going to be the "loser" in a dynamic, they will clutch at their previous gains and throw in conditions that were never on the table to begin with in order to still feel like they are "winners." Have you heard something like this before? "Well, okay, if you want to play with that person on your own, then you have to prepare my meals/ shine my boots/ clean my house/ let me fuck whomever I want for the next week."

How do we know when we are being misled by the Aggressive negotiator? After all part of the fun of being kinkier is the power dynamic exchange between the Mistress and slave. We love that position and the manipulation of power—the perceived imbalance of it all. And let me tell you, the Aggressive negotiator can appear to be the biggest, baddest, hottest Dominant in the room! It is really hot to know you are with a partner who is the Alpha. But being a Dominant and being abusive are two different things, even if the Alpha characteristics appear to blur that line initially. If you are a submissive and have an Alpha woman Dominant and she gives you the time to express your concerns and listens carefully, then it is more likely that you are going to continue to be with her than if she was just acting like a greedy pig without taking your feelings and desires into account. What if you recognize that this style is part of your own personality? Stay with me and I'll show you how to open up and become a more well-rounded person who can negotiate more successfully later in this chapter. First, let's look at the second negotiating type: the Passive negotiator.

The Passive negotiator is the flip side of the Aggressive negotiator in that he believes there will always be winners and losers in any negotiation and he focuses so much on not losing what he currently has that he doesn't believe he can be a "winner" at all. These are the types of people who allow the Aggressive negotiator to chip away at any sort of gains they have made for themselves and will bail when they feel it is happening. It can be like dealing with a little bunny who is quite shy and would rather run away and hide than have his or her desires and needs fulfilled or be eaten by the big bad Dominant. These individuals don't deal well with confrontation and tend to

How to assemble a fucking machine

1 This is the travel model of a fucking machine. All of the components, including the motor, fit into a small travel case. 2 There are only three parts that need to be assembled—the two shafts thread together and the dildo slips over the end. 3 The controller fits into your hand and you are good to go. It's that easy! (Slut not included.)

Vampire role play has become hotter over the past few years.

isolate themselves away from others and feel quite alone in their desires and too scared to share them with a partner. Have you heard this before? "I don't need any community. I just do my own thing my own way because no one would really understand my needs or desires." Or "I tried doing some of those things that my last Dominant really wanted but I got bored quickly and I found they really weren't validating my feelings." The Passive negotiator can be just as tricky to deal with as the Aggressive negotiator because you will spend most of your time chasing him before he opens up about what his needs and desires really are. He can also come off as really whiny and needy. This annoys the shit out of everyone in the end. What if you recognize yourself here? Pay extra attention to the best type of negotiating style: the Ingenious negotiator.

The Ingenious negotiator is ideal because if she isn't getting what she wants, she can adapt her behavior with her partner's needs in mind in order to pursue their long term goals. Think of an Ingenious negotiator as a cross-country adventurer. She will arm herself with a compass, a map, maybe some power bars and a little water bottle full of lube and she is going to get to where she wants to go regardless of the terrain. She quickly recognizes that there are many more paths to making both parties happy and satisfied beyond just "winners and losers." Fording streams, scaling cliffs, and negotiating the jungle of sexuality she will come up with ingenious and creative solutions to the problems she and her partner are experiencing. She believes in a win/win strategy and can successfully adapt in a win/lose if it will put her and her partner in a better position in the near future. For example, if she has tried one type of situation and it isn't working, she's flexible enough to accommodate other possibilities. She believes in learning from her mistakes and sees that challenges should be faced as a couple in a relationship, not an object to be won or lost. You can recognize the Ingenious negotiator by her inclusive language. She wants the other person to be as much a part of the decision-making process as possible so that the outcome is fair.

A little hand lotion applied to the skin before you use duct tape for bondage will make the removal less painful.

Here is a great example of a situation two switch friends of mine have encountered and the solution that works for them. She is the Top, but has a long and delicious fantasy of being used in a gangbang and objectified in very rough sex with multiple partners. He happens to have a cuckold fantasy and is a bottomy switch. You would think that these two fantasies would dovetail nicely... As fantasies—for sure! You can get all nasty and sweaty in your fantasies and do things that you would never do in real life. However in the real world there are many other variables that require consideration—emotional needs, sexual needs, and physical needs. It really turned them on when they would talk about the fantasy during sex and they loved how hot the fantasy was: her being gangbanged with him cuckolded in the corner. Throughout the workday they would melt the text screen of their cell phones chatting dirtily about it back and forth and they used it as a way to rev each other up for play, but they just couldn't bring themselves to do it in real life. It was too much of a leap. They had always been monogamous, both physically and emotionally, and they couldn't figure out how to tie their fantasy to real life since there are some very real issues involved in making such dreams come true. How would they establish the ground rules and what would those ground rules look like? How would they deal with any emotional fallout that might occur afterward?

They came to me and asked how they could navigate this so that they could have their fantasy needs met while at the same time negotiating a real-life encounter. I suggested something that was quite obvious to me but not to them—the cornerstone of these fantasies was objectification, both passive and active. She wanted to be gangbanged and be active in the objectification and he wanted to be passively cuckolded in the corner. I recommended that they ask another couple to come and join them in some play at their home but not touch or be sexually involved with each other. To know they could have an audience and turn them on as much as they were turning themselves on was something that hadn't occurred to them. In their fantasy life they were ready to be each other's dirty little sex puppets but the real-life issues they had were too much to bring to reality. So they compromised and found a middle ground that they could both enjoy and relish. He wound up locked into a chastity device and giving her oral sex while she kept up the dirty talk and told him how the other couple was going to fuck the shit out of her while he helplessly watched. That worked for both of them since they found a couple that was really into voyeurism, who liked watching them. Everybody won and to this day they all still get together to play separately but in the same room.

The Ingenious negotiator is not a pushover or willing to capitulate every time a new challenge arises; on the contrary he is as much about giving as receiving. You will find that these individuals will take over in some specific situations, such as when time and outcome is a factor, maybe at a fetish night when he and his partner find some hot new thing to take home to enjoy together, or if someone outside the relationship is directly challenging the hierarchy of the primary relationship. He tends to be flexible and ingenious.

The strengths of Ingenious negotiators are: they avoid trivial conflict as long as the other party is seeking a peaceful resolution, they value co-operation; if provoked they are quick to act against a move that is damaging to the relationship by letting the other party know immediately but they also forgive if the other person is sincere about his or her apology. Ingenious negotiators know that the core of all negotiation is trust and co-operation. They try to understand the other person's position and strive together toward a strategy that works for both people.

A package of 100 bamboo skewers is cheap and offers limitless fun for the masochist.

Facing Page: Some scenes, like medical scenarios, definitely benefit from lots of equipment.

If you have a gag in your partner, give him something to hold and drop that will make noise if he can't say his safeword, like a small bell.

In which prototype to you most see yourself? Which would you *want* to be? Two of them have their own particular appeal but in my experience the Ingenious negotiator is the one who understands the other's needs and desires and works to a resolution that satisfies everyone in the relationship. There will be times when all three will overlap but if you take time to figure out which one you are dealing with, you will be better equipped when it comes time to figuring out what you and your partner want and how you can both have it. Having introduced the three different types of negotiating styles, let's look more closely at understanding what types you and your partner might be. In getting kinkier we play with a power exchange that is hot, steamy and sometimes fraught with emotional and relationship landmines that aren't as apparent in vanilla relationships, and understanding these negotiating styles can help defuse them.

Outside the Boundaries and Emotional Landmines

Being able to communicate with your partner and also listen to what her needs are is the basis for negotiation. If you are a well-balanced person who can negotiate what your limits are and have them respected, all the while being able to get your needs met and your partner's needs met, this will set you up for more advanced, kinkier play down the road. But what if your kink, the thing that really gets you off, is past the limits of your partner? What about fantasies that are beyond reality, such as sex with aliens or other unrealistic fantasies that will probably never be actualized?

Even in the best of circumstances negotiations can be tricky. How do you tell someone your most deeply held desire when he only has half his attention on you because the kids are in the other room jumping on the couch or arguing over the Wii controller? When is the right time to bare your soul and expose the deepest fantasy you have always wanted to share but were afraid to? Setting up the right time to talk about what you like and want and being able to listen effectively to your partner requires that you pick the right time and the right place to discuss it, without distractions. If someone is going to share their deepest, darkest secrets with you, don't you think they should have your undivided attention? It might be a desire that is commonplace to you, but for someone who is confessing or giving voice to their secret desire for the first time, it takes a tremendous amount of courage to share. I am going to assume you are well past the

When you play with bondage in the pool, use nylon rope and don't be too rough.

Sometimes all a girl needs is a black pair of heels to be irresistable.

"newbie" stage. Maybe you have seen something new or there is something that has come up for you while you've been exploring, something you didn't even know you were curious about until you saw it demonstrated at an event, heard it talked about at a munch, or watched it online. That happens all the time—when you first get kinky, you are just starting to scratch the surface of your desires. Digging in deeper, after you have established trust and communication with your partner(s), is when the real fun begins! It is time to explore all sorts of nooks and crannies in your psyche and you want to know your partner is going to be along for the ride. Oftentimes your partner might not be into what you really enjoy and don't worry, it happens. It might be beyond his comfort level—say, having a single-tail whip used on him, or indulging in messy food play. There are things you can do to approach this:

■ Find someone else to do it (with your partner's consent and boundaries in place).

■ Get there together. Sometimes bringing in a friend who is more experienced to demonstrate or show you the ropes can be a great way to ease both of you into something new, and then you both go on to explore.

There is also a popular trend in sexual therapy popularized by Austrian sex educators Professor Bernhard Ludwig and Dr. Ulrike Brandenburg that concentrates on two key points in human sexual relationships that I feel work very well for Kink: the negotiated favor and "If you don't feel like sex but your partner does—try it anyway."

The good doctors feel you can bargain with things that aren't even sexual in nature. It doesn't have to be "an evening of spankings for an evening of ball gags." If you knew you would be able to hog-tie your partner and spend an evening trying out all sizes of butt plugs and other fun things that go into squirmy people—would it be worth doing it to her if you did the dishes or took the dog for a walk ahead of time so she isn't stressing about these tasks? Men are very direct with our approach—stimulus/response. Women on the other hand need more time and their foreplay can start from the time you finish until the next time. Create a comfortable environment and you may have her purring in your hands.

The next point they stress is that we don't always feel like sex. Sometimes we feel just "meh" but our partner is horny and ready to go! In a way, isn't it flattering to know that you just hanging around in your jammies and eating

Avoid striking someone on his joints or bony parts. Stick to the fleshy areas like the bum, upper thighs, and upper back.

Before using hot wax, rub lotion all over the skin.

chips on the couch while watching TV can get him hot? Take it as a compliment and get naked together and have some fun! Look at it this way: you don't like working out, but once you get your gym clothes on and push some weights or run some laps, you usually feel wonderful afterward and glad you did it; most of the time, anyway. The same goes for playtime and sex. Once you get into something or someone you usually have a great time. Keep in mind this is only applicable if you are ambivalent and could go either way; I am not condoning nonconsensual pressure. Consent is key!

Kink Fatigue

When you are getting kinkier, you might find old interests falling by the wayside and other times you might be stuck in a rut. You know the kind, where you both enjoy the same things over and over again and you both feel you want to learn some new things. There is a solution—the kink conference. There are a great many kinky conventions across the world. Lots of us Kinksters, including me, attend to both teach and learn how other Kinky people do things. And we can pick and choose what we might want to add to suit our relationships best, or even enhance them. For many people who are excited about exploring and evolving in their relationships this is an exciting time. I love attending conventions and workshops, both as a presenter and as an attendee. I find that the more I learn and grow on my own, the more I realize other people do things differently and similar and sometimes with just a bit of a tweak to what I do and that helps my own playtime evolution. Whenever I think I have seen or heard it all, someone comes up with something exciting and new. That is part of the excitement—BDSM (in its conventional terms) and power play has been a part of the human experience for thousands of years, but the Internet has brought it to the masses in the past fifteen years. The organization and acceleration of its distribution is currently in a golden age, one that I revel in, and I look forward to seeing what will happen next.

They say there is nothing new under the sun; only the way YOU do it is different. At Kink events you will witness a lot of things in workshops and demonstrations and will probably want to incorporate some of these into your relationship. However there is *so* much that happens at an event

Facing Page: Chains can help keep your sub exactly where you want them.

Skintight latex is fabulously sexy whether you're wearing it or just lucky enough to watch.

that there is a definite sensory and cognitive overload. When you get home and try to incorporate these new things into your relationship, some things work, some partly work, and sometimes none of it works and feelings get hurt and the emotional stability of the relationship becomes shaky, with each person feeling the other is at fault. New techniques can cause instability if not introduced properly and within the correct context. Emotions can run high when rules change and reactions can become overreactions, which then cause an even bigger chasm in the communication between two people. This happens. It isn't just YOU. The process of introducing new concepts and ideas and changing some established patterns isn't something to be done on a whim with your Kinky partner. But sometimes they are necessary to avoid Kink fatigue—to keep things exciting and fresh. There are other times when we find something new and love it so much we focus only on it and in doing so, cause it to fail instead of thoughtfully negotiating with our partner and figuring out how to make it work effectively.

What do you do when things go sideways and don't work out like you assumed they would? If you are the one responsible for introducing the new technique or rule or whatever it is you want to do differently, and your partner tried her best, you have to be willing to admit that something isn't working and talk about it in a context away from your Kinky lifestyle. Move outside the dungeon or bedroom—having a neutral place to discuss the issue like adults is going to help bring both of you closer. If you are accountable, admit it and try to figure out what the next steps are you should both take to make the new play work. Being willing to say, "Hey, I was wrong, I thought this might enhance what we have but it clearly isn't working for both of us. Let's talk about what we can do to either salvage it or chuck it," will make your partner respect you more than if you just said nothing and let it chip away at the trust you have both built.

As time passes you will likely want to go deeper with your D/s relationship. You might want to explore the Mistress/slave aspect of ownership and this takes an enormous amount of trust and a leap of faith based on you both having a solid idea of where you want to go with your relationship and how that perceived power imbalance will work. However, there are pitfalls that can throw the other person off balance, cause hurt and confusion and sometimes derail the relationship. How do we successfully

Know who you are playing with.

Use a variety of instruments on your slave. She deserves it after all!

deal with fundamental changes or introducing new elements into a relationship without the other person feeling compromised or betrayed? We will attempt to answer those questions in the following chapter: Roles Taken Further.

Five Key Points for Advanced Negotiation with Your Partner:

■ Talk with your partner about both your needs on a regular basis to keep communication fluid and dynamic.

■ Be willing to see the other person's side.

■ Learn the three types of negotiators—Aggressive, Passive and Ingenious.

■ Recognize when to make concessions and when to stand firm.

■ Be open-minded enough to try something your partner wants as long as it doesn't compromise your safety or security.

Chapter Three

Roles Taken Further

Not everyone is lucky enough to understand how delicious it is to suffer.
—Katharine Hepburn

What is the difference between fun bedroom games and a lifestyle choice? How do you know if you are ready for a Master/slave relationship and are capable of maintaining it through the endless detours, emotional demands or maybe even geographic location issues? Some people see M/s as the ultimate level in any sort of BDSM relationship, as if the Dominant and submissive should be constantly working toward a goal of a Master/slave relationship—and for many that *is* an ultimate goal. Others enjoy occasional role-playing bedroom romps or some D/s in their lives; there is a clear difference between that and a formally structured M/s relationship. In this chapter I will try to help you figure out what you ultimately want for an M/s relationship—are you looking for a play/part-time relationship or a full-time M/s relationship?—and how to negotiate that goal with someone you care about.

The clear delineation between bedroom roles and M/s can be explained easily enough. In a light D/s or kinky structure, roles sometimes drop when real life intrudes in ways that can ruin your sexy time, e.g., picking up the kids from school, finding out the dog just threw up all over your new rug, or maybe an incident involving your mother, a lasagna and a surprise visit on a Tuesday night while you and your partner are dressed up like the Gimp from *Pulp Fiction* (don't ask, my mother was traumatized for a month). The roles you and your partner use and play with can be dropped at times of

Facing Page: Bad puppy boy!

51

Giving yourself over completely to a mistress can be intimidating, but also infintely rewarding.

crisis when you both put on your vanilla faces and deal with those issues and crises and the vanillas of the world never need to know what it is you like to do in the bedroom. This works well for lots of people who prefer to turn their D/s roles on and off as the situation requires. Other people feel a calling toward a full-time Mistress/slave relationship and the structure that it entails. This lifestyle choice is one where you let the essence of your role define how you conduct yourself with your partner. As a couple or poly family (more on poly in the next chapter) you use your roles to help define your boundaries as a full-time M/s dynamic. Time, distance and opportunities might be cause for a M/s relationship being only part-time or play based. I have been involved in a couple of long-distance relationships with slave-oriented people over the years and while we were only together part-time because of the distance, every time we got together it was a full-time M/s relationship. Let me say that again in case I have confused you, it confused me at first: you can work on your M/s dynamic in a part-time capacity if you are apart, but every time you are together you are full time. This would be considered a play-based M/s relationship. How they act and react to your needs as the Mistress during the time they are with you can bring a lot of fulfillment to their role and to yours. Rituals can help you both stay connected and deepen that connection as a play-based relationship, especially if distance is the largest hurdle to overcome. Once you have figured out if you desire a part-time or a full-time M/s relationship and you are developing it, let me encourage you to value discretion in public. Our goal is not to make the vanillas uncomfortable in everyday society with our dynamics; you don't have to let the world know you are in a Master/slave relationship, but in everyday situations where immediate decisions are needed, the slave always defers to the Master or Mistress.

Bruising time can be reduced by using Arnica cream.

Are You Ready to Move into a M/s Relationship?

Picture this: you have been involved in a long-term kinky D/s relationship. In the beginning things were exciting and hot but after a year or two your interest has waned. Things you both were really excited about and would get naked in a heartbeat for now have lost a little bit of their sparkle. How do you regain that feeling of excitement? How do you put things back on track so you can both move to the next level of a M/s relationship? In the last chapter we looked at more advanced negotiation: how to communicate

If you do needle play, keep your sharps container nearby for proper disposal.

your desires to your partner and understand what theirs are, even if they don't sync up. When you have someone you feel is ready to explore a M/s with you, the foundation of your dynamic should include the following:

- The ability to trust
- The ability to negotiate with compassion
- Inherent respect for yourself and your partner
- The ability to see challenges as a learning opportunity
- The ability to creatively set scenarios and activities
- An understanding of protocol, etiquette and manners to help guide each other

It doesn't seem as if M/s has the exclusive rights to these points, does it? Wouldn't you value almost all of these in a vanilla relationship?

I don't know if anyone can truly know if they are ready for a Master/slave relationship until they embark upon one. Ignorance is bliss for those who jump into it without thought, but I knew I had to overcome emotional walls I've put up over the years in order to truly commit to it. I opened my heart to it and let my guard down, and embraced the unknown. The trust and vulnerability involved are arguably my biggest kinks. It's what I get off on the most about this type of relationship; in my opinion, without it, there is no M/s dynamic.

For some there is a strict line between "play" and regular life; the two never cross, they don't mix, they get turned on (and off) like a tap. My world doesn't work that way, I'm a service-oriented slave and that's just who I am. Don't get me wrong, I don't stop in Walmart to kiss Master's boots, but the dynamic is there. It's everywhere I go. This is how I demonstrate my love for the dynamic, not a mask to wear on weekends.

—Elle, Lifestyle Slave

What do you need to know about a M/s relationship? First of all the roles should help define and enhance your life rather than control it. You might really enjoy the structure it brings to your experiences. If you are unowned, not having a Master doesn't make you less of a slave. In fact being a single submissive or slave gives you the opportunity for growth—to

Facing Page: A good slave knows her place.

Vacuum beds are perfect for teasing and tantalizing your play partners.

sharpen or pick up new skill sets that will enhance your Mistress's life when she finally does find you. Likewise if you are a Mistress in search of a slave you can use your single life to sharpen your skills by taking classes or networking with other people in M/s relationships to pick their brains and see what works and doesn't work for them. Some very good friends of mine, a M/s couple, took a long time to explore and figure out what they wanted in their M/s relationship. Their M/s structure evolved at a rate that was comfortable for them. They started off as a Dominant and submissive and as they learned and grew together they started tapping other

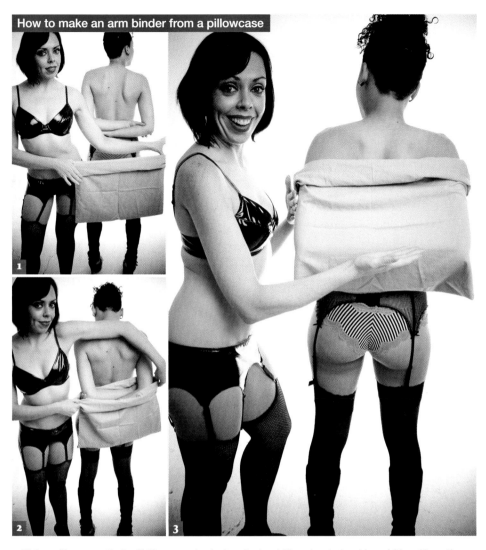

How to make an arm binder from a pillowcase

1 Pick a pillowcase that will fit your submissive. It should be about shoulder width. **2** Have them fold their arms behind them... **3** and slip it up to their shoulders. If you seat the arms right at the bottom of the case they won't be able to get out.

people in the scene about what M/s structures worked for them and why. Growing and learning together with what the Mistress knew she wanted and the structure that she wanted to have in place gave them both time to work up toward their ultimate goal of M/s. It has taken years, and they are constantly evolving as they continue to explore together. She serves her Mistress exactly as the Mistress desires and all of her decision-making ability is deferred to the Mistress. There are daily and weekly protocols

that the slave follows with punishments handed out if she fails in her duties. When you are ready to explore this type of relationship, consistency in your behavior and expectation is key to ensuring you build a strong foundation for both of you. The Master or Mistress is in charge of creating the structure, environment and parameters, and the slave is responsible for serving to the best of her ability.

There are a lot of M/s and D/s conferences that you can attend across the world that will help give you ideas and tips on how to structure your M/s relationship. Each one has its own flavor and focus. Some are structured primarily as Mistress or Master/slave retreats, others are set up to promote the Leather lifestyle, and still others cater to the pansexual community. If you attend them you will find some of the same presenters and teachers at various venues. Usually their classes will be different as they cater to the focus of the event. For example, at one event I might present a workshop on "Dynamic Problem Solving with Rope," and at another "How to Kinkify Your Partner: Advice for Newbies." Presenters want to maximize their exposure and their knowledge base so they have to be able to present on a variety of different topics, provided they are qualified to do so. Pick their brains after a class that you enjoyed—ask them what activities work best for them when you go to M/s conferences. How do they make it work and what activities do they use to do so? What type of structure do they employ and how do they keep that spark alive in a relationship where the power dynamic is so heavily loaded on one person?

Having the chance to speak with like minded-people who are in M/s relationships or are considering it is a very valuable way to get feedback and figure out what is working for them and how you might best decide for yourselves if a full-time M/s dynamic is for both of you. Ultimately, you are the ones that have to make that decision. Ask yourself questions such as, "Is my partner not only trustworthy but does he take my feelings and needs into account as I am entering into a slavery agreement with him?" or "As a slave, what opportunities do I have to voice my opinion in a respectful way that will ensure I am heard?" or "What will our relationship look like and how will it operate in private and in public?" M/s is about enhancing your lives, not about the sole domination of one individual over the other where your concerns or needs are stamped on with

If you are going to play with medical staples, DON'T forget to buy the staple remover at the same time....

Facing Page: Be a good girl and stay where your mistress puts you.

The good thing about latex outfits is you can layer upon it. Here is a catsuit with a corset on top.

Strong women are sexy!

her size 7 stilettos. After you have asked yourself the pertinent questions and you feel you are ready for a M/s relationship, let me show you how to negotiate introducing it.

Negotiating with the Three Cs

Clarity, Communication and Consistency: in this type of relationship, just as in a vanilla relationship, communication is a two-way street. It requires active listening and Communicating to ensure Clarity. Consistency isn't something that lies solely with the Dominant or just on the slave's shoulders. Owning another person is a great responsibility and it requires both parties to be clear about what they are looking for and how they hope to achieve those goals. It requires understanding the actions of your partner but also understanding the motivations behind her needs and desires. It is easy to just live in a fantasy world for the weekend, a long weekend or maybe even a week or a month, letting all of your fantasies come true with your very own dirty little sex puppet. These times are great and I do encourage you to treat each other like dirty little sex puppets; get sticky, worn out, bruised and exhausted! Yet there is going to come a time when you

If a scene goes sideways, don't panic.

have to return to reality, and you will need to develop some skills so you can evolve past the obvious sexualized relationship into something that has a broader scope as a lifestyle relationship. Consistency in behaviors and expectations will assist in this transition.

My own experience at owning slaves started as a long-distance relationship. We both found it was easy to shack up for a week-long sexual adventure at a cabin in the woods. Chaining her to the fieldstone fireplace and doing whatever I wanted with a whole bag full of toys was hot and delicious. But as we became more involved, particularly with some very strong emotions, I found that consistency was the strongest foundation in facilitating the M/s portion of the relationship, even from a distance. There should be real life rewards and real life punishments. A Master or Mistress should be able to command from a distance but the ultimate goal would be to both be closer and immerse yourselves into a 27/4 relationship where the distance isn't an issue. We found that for us, back in our salad days, the fantasy of long term M/s could run into some real life challenges. How are you going to deal with a slave that is in another city who doesn't write the prescribed passages in her slave journal? What if the slave is reluctant to accept punishment that you have explained carefully and is required? How do you cope with real life intrusions into someone's service to you? It was hard at first for me but since I have been through it and hit many speed bumps along the way in my learning process, I am going to show you what I think is the best way to make it work out for everyone.

It is always easier to deal with a fantasy than real life. Real life is tough. Real life involves bills, the dog that needs to go out, a partner that might be away on business trips, children's needs, et cetera. It is hard enough in this day and age to schedule private sexy time with each other, with all of the demands that are made on us, and when we DO get that time, we want to spend it in heavy playtime. But reality does come knocking and we CAN negotiate it by incorporating M/s into our lives. Understanding your partner's motivation for his interests and the role you play in facilitating those interests and fantasies, and establishing clear expectations of what you both need to do to keep the dynamic strong will reassure your slave when you are away and will give him comfort and reassurance that he is consistently serving you even if you aren't physically present.

Let's take a closer look at how these roles can help enhance your life, and what you should and shouldn't do while conducting yourself in the

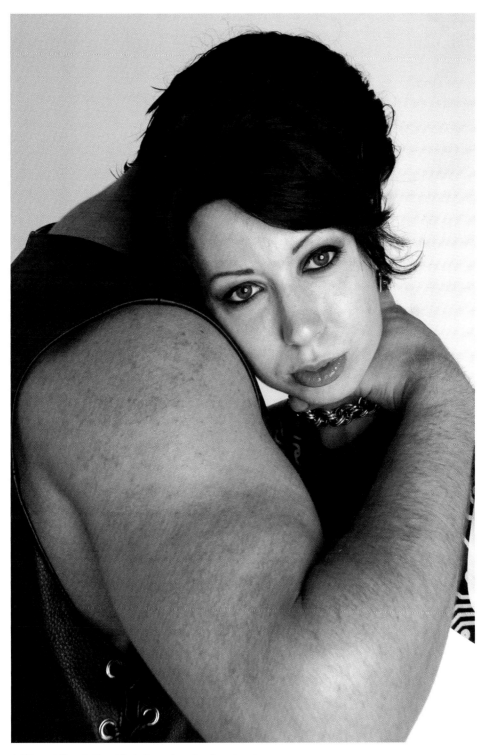

A D/s or M/s relationship is based on trust and caring.

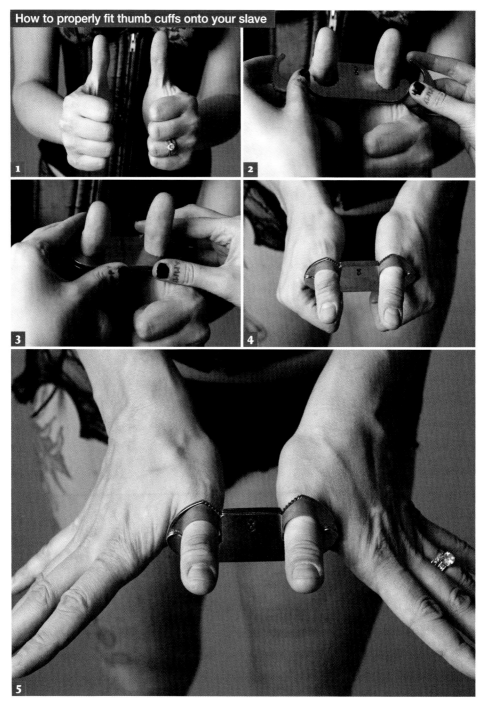

How to properly fit thumb cuffs onto your slave

1 Get a pair of willing thumbs. 2 Fasten the cuffs around the thumbs until firm, but not too tight. 3 Click them into place. 4 Make sure you monitor their circulation; thumb cuffs can be particularly nasty for this. 5 Enjoy them all captured but don't yank them by the cuffs.

everyday world. If you are a Dominant or Master, keep in mind that you may have a dominant personality but you are "a Dominant" to just your partner. If you treat other people in the general public in the same manner you might treat your slave, it will come off as pushy and rude and you will be taken for a jerk. You might be the alpha male in the pack or you might be the Queen Bitch of Lower Germania but the lady at the grocery store doesn't need to hear how special you are when you order her to "Double bag it now!" at the end of her long shift. Conducting yourself with grace and dignity never goes out of style and if you feel that M/s is for you, then you should use the best parts of that structure to not only enhance your life but others' as well. A Mistress can conduct herself with a smile on her face in the public eye; can be confident, considerate and warm to those she meets on a daily basis while still maintaining her role. A Mistress or Master is there to enhance others' lives by providing a certain amount of structure for themselves, which in turn can assist those in need. It can be something as simple as being a good and compassionate person who helps others in times of distress. You aren't less of a Master for holding open a door for an elderly lady leaving the grocery store; you aren't less of a Mistress for offering to help a new mother with some laundry and tidying her house; you aren't less of a Master or Mistress for offering to stand in to run a munch for someone while he is away on vacation. Rather, you should strive to be a composed, compassionate person who can make a difference by showing respect and compassion to others. If you are a slave in search of a Master of worth, how would you feel if you saw Him helping a single mother change her flat tire? What would you think if your Mistress stopped to give directions to lost tourists in your town? Would you think less of them because they care or would you feel that your slavery is in the hands of a good, competent and responsible person? Would the aura that shines around them shine a little brighter that day for you?

Of course it would.

We all want someone who is respectful, compassionate and inviting to enhance our lives. An M/s relationship is no different; it's just that the boundaries and expectations are more strongly defined between the two people. Let's look at some issues that you need to be aware of, patterns that I have seen time and time again in the evolution from a D/s to a M/s relationship, so that you can recognize them when they start to rear their heads in your relationship and learn how to successfully navigate through them.

Play should be fun but safety should be serious.

The crank neck vibrator is great for hitting the G-spot and learning how to squirt.

Slavery: Starting Slow and Keeping the Excitement

Let's assume you are ensconced in a new M/s or D/s relationship. It is natural for you to be excited. You want to share with your friends and colleagues: "Look I have a new Master and we are so happy together, everything is perfect!" One of the great joys in BDSM comes when you find someone to complement your kinky life. But after six months the initial excitement starts to wear off and reality starts showing through the seams in the curtain. Next thing you realize, neither of you is as focused as you were in the beginning. You may be frustrated if the relationship isn't meeting your initial expectations. Ultimately we are human and this is a pattern of typical human relationships regardless of the power dynamic. When you are new to each other and the dynamic is still fluid and exiting, you are both ready to explore deeply and want everything to be perfect. So how do you build and maintain the excitement without having your expectations crash down around you a year into the relationship? I believe that when two people enter into a M/s dynamic, they should start off slow and establish clear expectations. You may want to be chained to her desk all day long with her initials branded into your butt, but let's take some time to get there, okay? You CAN get there, but a slave and a Mistress both need to be aware of not going too far too fast, regardless of how hot it is at the time. It is easier to explore slowly and dial it back than to move too fast and wind up with a mess on your hands (literally as well as metaphorically). Ever try to catch a basket full of apples that are falling through your hands? You grab one or two but the rest wind up a big mess on the floor. We don't want the slave's or Master's emotional landscape to look like a finger painting done by Jackson Pollock in his kindergarten class, so lets just ease into things and if you run into speed bumps along the way, it will be easier to deal with them one at a time, rather than encountering a multitude of problems all at once.

Routine and frequent assessment is a great place to start. It also provides a foundation upon which you can build further down the road when you want to introduce new aspects or activities. A simple assessment requirement could be as easy as "I will be looking at your slave journal every fourth time we get together to see if you have completed the homework I have assigned to you." Or "I expect you to shave your pubic hair regularly and will be checking each day/once a week." Assessing your "property" or partner requires diligence and the responsibility to back up your requirements with

Use condoms on insertable toys for easier and faster cleanup.

67

Casual play
partners are
entitled to
respect.

actual consequences to reinforce behavior. Good behavior is rewarded and bad behavior is simply not tolerated and should be swiftly corrected.

A note on slave journals: having your slave keep a journal provides him with a space for reflection and examination of his feelings and actions and reactions. This can provide a lot of feedback for the Mistress and the slave should be working toward transparency in the journal just as a solid M/s relationship is built upon transparency. It takes time to get there and sometimes slaves will be unsure if they should record the way they really feel about their experiences with their M/s relationship and let me reassure you that positive or negative feedback is essential for that relationship to evolve and grow. If I have a slave keep a journal, I desire the unedited view of her emotions and feelings. I can see what is working, what isn't, and what might be sharpened and polished to a keen edge. What I don't use a journal for is as an excuse for punishment. I would never go through it and pick out something to punish a slave for having written, unless it was an assignment that was not completed. Never punish a slave for his feelings, work with his emotions so that you both can have a clearer sense of the relationship. Journaling has worked so well for me that I recommend to every slave I meet that he or she should be keeping one for their Master. Sometimes slaves who cannot articulate their concerns well, do very well with listing them logically in a journal when they have time to reflect in their downtime, without the pressure of their Masters standing over them demanding that their latest homework assignment be completed in a half hour.

When Roles Spill Over

Be careful about being so wrapped up in your lifestyle that you are intrusive into the lives of vanilla people, especially in providing explanations for them. Perhaps your new slave makes you so happy that you are bursting with joy and want to tell the world and live it 24/7. This is natural, but still your mother doesn't need to be introduced to your new slave with an explanation like, "Mom this is my new slave Jeff, please don't mind that he is eating off the floor tonight for dinner." Mom doesn't want to know her that her baby girl is not only into owning another human being but likes to make him eat off the floor as punishment for not performing proper foot worship earlier. Would you ever ask Mom if she takes a load on her face from your father?

Nipples are more resilient than you might think.

Yoga is great for
enabling
submissives and
bottoms to stay
flexible for
extended
bondage scenes.

No, I didn't think so.

Master and slavery is about intent and the enhancement of life, not about forcing your will or lifestyle upon those who would require a lengthy explanation. Vanilla people are curious and will more than likely ask questions about your lifestyle if you choose to share it with them. Give them open and honest answers, but keep in mind the audience you are addressing. The vanillas probably don't need to hear the super-juicy details about the size of dildo you have trained your slave to take up his butt while he sleeps on the floor under your bed, but they might be less shocked if you say, "Oh, I have my lover sleep on the floor when he stays over." Discretion is the better part of being a role model and as our scene and lifestyle continues to grow, we want there to be less friction between the vanillas and ourselves. No one needs to know the most intimate details of your life. What you do consensually in the privacy of your own home is your business and is no one else's. If the vanillas are asking prying questions that you are not comfortable with answering, deflect them with grace and dignity and a gentle smile on your face.

Most of the Masters and Mistresses and slaves I know that are in successful long-term relationships, don't appear on the outside to the vanilla world as anything other than "normal" couples, whether or not they live together. A slave doesn't have to say, "Let me ask my Master if I can work late," to his boss. Saying, "Let me call my husband/boyfriend/girlfriend/wife and find out if they have something on for tonight," gets the point across without non-consensually involving the vanillas. Mainstream society may not understand and making them uncomfortable should not be our goal. Choosing your words carefully can help keep unnecessary questions that you would rather not answer at bay. On the other hand, when you get together with other M/s couples you can revel in the slaves sitting on the floor at the Mistresses' feet, or serving and fetching, and relax with the playtime that can go on around you at a private function, particularly at one of my favorites: the High Protocol Event. It is a lot of fun being around other like-minded adults for an evening in a club; a weekend retreat is a great way to keep things fun and fresh. I like to make sure that if I have someone personally serving me, after the event I provide them with the

Facing Page: Vetwrap bandaging tape is stretchy, sticks only to itself and comes in lots of pretty colours.

time and environment to communicate their reflections on the experience either in a journal or by discussion. For some Mistresses or Masters this may go against the 24/7 model of M/s, but I challenge any Master or Mistress out there to tell me that their submissive or slave's concerns are not taken into consideration in making decisions for the relationship. Any loving and caring BDSM relationship will always have the other person's best interests at heart. I always want to know what worked for them, what didn't, how they felt and if their motivations for the weekend altered or strengthened while at an event with me. Owning someone or being owned takes a great deal of trust, patience and dedication to help that other person shine and enhance their life. There was an event I attended in the summer where the goal of the weekend away with other M/s couples was to be a High Protocol weekend. Expectations, boundaries and rules were strict and clear and the slaves were meant to follow them and the Masters and Mistresses were to enforce their adherence to the High Protocol theme. Flowers were cut daily and to exact lengths for the dining room table, the rooms were cleaned and prepped every morning, wood was chopped to exact dimensions, feet were licked, massages were given and it was all with a High Protocol flair. It was a very relaxing weekend for the Master and Mistresses and for the slaves it was a lot of work, but work that they felt satisfied in performing to exacting standards. This weekend worked very well because of the guidelines of Protocol, Etiquette and Manners were laid out beforehand so that all parties knew what the expectations were. In any M/s structure, Protocol, Etiquette and Manners will be beneficial and offer a strong support structure for your M/s relationship.

Protocol, Etiquette and Manners

Protocol is a set of conventions that dictates how a person is to act in a given situation. Etiquette is how you act in that situation and manners are how you react when others don't follow those conventions. Established M/s relationships that work well will have a strong element of all of these three in them. A Master or Mistress is always in control. Their slave or submissive is a direct reflection of their influence on and training of their charge. If a slave steps out of line in his or her behavior, it reflects poorly on the Dominant. Likewise if you have an issue with a slave who you feel may have been rude or exhibited any other undesired behavior, you would not approach

Be creative when finding new things to use as tit clamps.

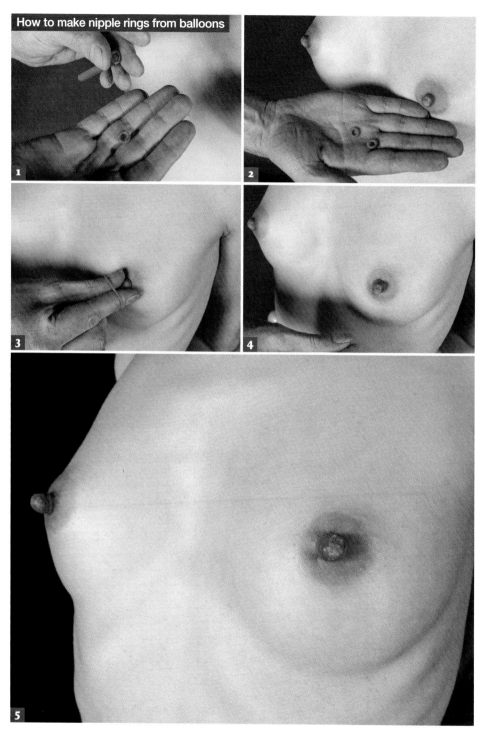

How to make nipple rings from balloons

1 Tear or snip the ends off circus balloons. 2 Line them up. 3 Slip one over your thumb and forefinger and pinch the nipple. 4 Then let them roll off and into place. 5 Yum.

Stockings show off your sub's sexy curves and always make a scene even hotter.

that slave and say, "I find your behavior rude," as he is a direct reflection of his Master's control. You instead must go to the Dominant and express your concern and possible displeasure. She might have many reasons or none at all for the slave's behavior; it is not up to us to decide. If a slave has been rude then it his Mistress who will mete out the punishment.

Oftentimes in our society you will find vanilla issues conflicting with a M/s dynamic. The Western world's values center on independency and assertiveness and this can be seen on the surface as in conflict with the polite subservience a Master would expect from those who are in service to him. A Master or Mistress should always be in control. He or she should be composed, calm, and not reactionary to extraneous outside forces that would cause a vanilla person to falter or stumble. But stumble we will at times, and being able to say, "I was wrong, I am accountable," will demonstrate the strength of your character if indeed you are at fault. Similarly, forgiveness of the shortcomings of others is a hallmark of a strong character. A M/s relationship is governed by certain levels of protocol. Protocol not only gives slaves the outline for acceptable and unacceptable behavior in a situation; it also gives Dominants an understanding of how their slaves

Finishing the ends of your rope with whipping thread will make it easier to pull it through tight spots.

Silicone toys can go in the dishwasher.

and other slaves are to act in any situation.

There are three levels of protocol essential to a healthy, functioning M/s dynamic:

Low: This is where day-to-day and vanilla life appear the closest. A collar may or may not be worn; it might involve grocery shopping, laundry, picking the kids up at daycare, et cetera. Vanillas would not normally be able to immediately discern that there is an M/s dynamic functioning other than one partner doting on another.

Mid: This is a level of protocol for public BDSM-centered functions, such as a fetish night party. The slave would be given instructions ahead of time as to what is expected of him, such as fetching drinks, waiting in line for the play equipment while the Mistress socializes, and acting in accord to their Master's desires. At this level it is clearly apparent through behavior and codified methods of attire that there is an M/s dynamic at work.

High: This is the most demanding level of protocol, usually used for short periods of time to demonstrate complete servitude. It might entail the serving of Afternoon or "High" Tea, where white gloves and a formal seating arrangement reflect the generosity of the host and well-trained slaves reflect a high degree of exact measure. High protocol is also used to demonstrate at a class or training function. This level of protocol is difficult to keep up for long periods of time because of the exacting standards. However for me it is a joy to see an exceptionally well-trained slave serve at a high protocol event. There is a spring in his step, his movements filled with purpose, and lightness in his heart when serving his Mistress in the most demanding way possible, where every detail is scrutinized and each and every movement is watched carefully. For a slave, there is no greater opportunity to demonstrate his love in public than this opportunity to demonstrate the skill sets that his Mistress has required him to achieve.

I have a very good friend who is a slave and the protocol his Mistress has set out for him includes writing in his journal every night and bowing on his hands and knees before a pair of her boots before climbing into bed. Part

Facing Page: Don't forget to restrain all parts of your submissives.

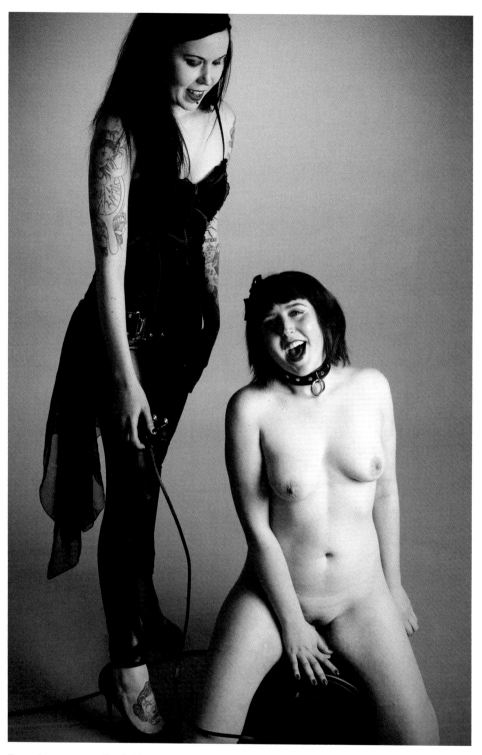

Forced orgasms on the Sybian are more fun than you can imagine!

of his etiquette with her is also having the chance to polish her boots before she arrives and then lacing them onto her when she is settled and comfortable. His manners are impeccable when he's out at a club whether or not his Mistress is with him. If others try to touch his collar or boss him around because he is a slave, he simply smiles and reminds them, "No touch, not yours." This is a nice, polite way of letting others know the boundaries that he and his Mistress have established. You will find that incorporating protocol, etiquette and manners into your M/s practice will provide you with the scaffolding to better structure the dynamic of your relationship and give you both a common language for understanding each other.

What happens if you have a solid one-on-one relationship—a Master with one slave—and you want to shift things into a more polyamorous relationship? What are the strengths and pitfalls of introducing new partners into your established dynamic and how do you do it successfully? If you want to have a stable or a Leather family you better get out your Blackberry's day timer because the logistics of a poly are much more intense than what you might be used to. In the following chapter we will explore the strengths and challenges of being polyamorous.

Use water-based lube on silicone toys, NOT silicone lube. Confusing but necessary.

Five Key Points for Taking Roles Further:

■ M/s is about enhancing your lives together.

■ A Master or Mistress is always in control of themselves.

■ A slave's behavior is a direct reflection of the influence a Master or Mistress has on him.

■ There are levels of protocol that will help frame your learning experiences.

■ Owning or being owned requires transparent communication between everyone involved.

Chapter Four

BDSM Play and Polyamorous Relationships

Passion makes the world go round. Love just makes it a safer place.
—Ice T

So you want to explore being polyamorous? Maybe you think you might already be polyamorous, but you're not sure how it works? What is the difference between having relationships with many people, as opposed to just playing and having sex with many people with no emotional attachment? This chapter looks at the subtle and not-so-subtle nuances of having more than one partner for play or relationships.

What are the benefits and challenges of being involved in a polyamorous relationship? Relationships with others are what bring us the most joy in life and also the most hardship. Life is fluid and dynamic, and we are constantly having new experiences that will color our future. When I think about arguments I have had with my partners and the challenges we have faced over the years, I realize that it is difficult enough managing one relationship; when you add one extra or a few more people, it can be a challenge that not everyone can cope with and few people on the outside can understand. However, the joys that can be experienced by sharing your love with more than one person can take you in directions that are incredibly

Facing Page: When it comes to submissives, two heads are always better than one.

A piece of string and a row of clothespins make for a great titty play toy called a zipper.

Try flogging with your other hand to build up your dexterity.

rewarding and enriching. Like all relationships, it only works if communication is transparent and open. This idea is at the heart of being polyamorous: open and transparent communication. Some people mistake polyamory merely for being "slutty." It doesn't mean that. If you want to go out and "slut it up" without any emotional attachment, then go directly to the portion of this chapter on open relationships and swinging. Being slutty is fun and you can explore all sorts of sexy adventures, but being poly doesn't always include that in its list of priorities. Inside the relationship, you can be slutty with those you love but not open to casual sexual encounters with people outside of your dynamic. Your sexual habits have to be secondary to being involved emotionally with more than one person, or else those close to you are going to get hurt.

Open or Closed?

Polyamorous doesn't always mean "open" and give you license to run around and have as many sexual partners as you like without taking into account the emotions and feelings of those you are involved with.

Each flogger will have different leather that will cause different sensations. This is deerskin and delivers a soft thud.

Polyamory is about connecting with one or more partners, each in his or her own individual way, on emotional as well as physical levels. It is a complex and interesting dynamic that can work wonderfully for the right people. It has enjoyed resurgence in popularity among the BDSM crowd because it allows for flexibility and variable interests. In chapter 2 we discussed the possibility of your primary partner not being comfortable exploring or participating in a new activity with you. If you are both open-minded enough, you can arrange for someone who *is* comfortable with this new direction to possibly join your romantic lives. It can enhance your dynamic and bring a lot to the table that can be beneficial to everyone, if this new arrangement is handled well. I have experienced various polyamorous relationships over the years and have enjoyed the benefits and also the challenges that those relationships have revealed.

One relationship I was in involved three others: my primary girlfriend/play partner, my submissive and my submissive's girlfriend. My girlfriend/play partner (who was a switch) and I welcomed a new person into our relationship who was a heavy masochist and a service-oriented submissive. The submissive also had a vanilla relationship with her girlfriend, who wasn't interested in kink or BDSM. While I wasn't intimately involved with the submissive's girlfriend on a sexual level, I was involved with her on a mental and emotional level because I had to consider her feelings while being involved with her girlfriend, as my girlfriend and I developed *our* relationship with the masochist. If you have two or more people in a relationship dynamic, and even if you are not involved with them directly, you still have a responsibility to that person's partner to treat their relationship with respect and dignity. I knew that if my primary and I were going to do something intense to my submissive that might put her in a very vulnerable position, either mentally or physically, we had to ensure that we wouldn't be downloading that luggage onto her girlfriend when she returned home. With greater play comes greater responsibility, and the last thing I would want is for someone else to have to clean up after an emotionally charged situation that I am responsible for. So in this situation, our downtime was important after playing, the time we devoted to cooling down after an intense scene and talking about things, rather than just asking the submissive to leave as soon as we were "finished" with her.

Handwriting a note telling your lover what you want to do to her and slipping it in her coat pocket is a great way to whet her sexual appetite.

Facing Page: Subs always look most delicious when they're on their knees.

A simple riding crop with some different ends can be enough fun for a whole day.

One thing I discovered when I first began my journey many years ago was that polyamory differs greatly depending on the people involved and how they want to define the relationship. It is important to identify what poly means for you and for others you become involved with so you will be able to navigate multiple partners—and juggle all of their schedules on your iPhone. The basic definition of polyamory is what tends to be the popular view: romantic love involving more than a couple. It can incorporate just one extra person or multiple additional partners, in an arrangement where everyone is on the same page and they all value communication, integrity and honesty. As simple as this definition sounds, it can become incredibly complex. If you are new to the kink world or just figuring out poly

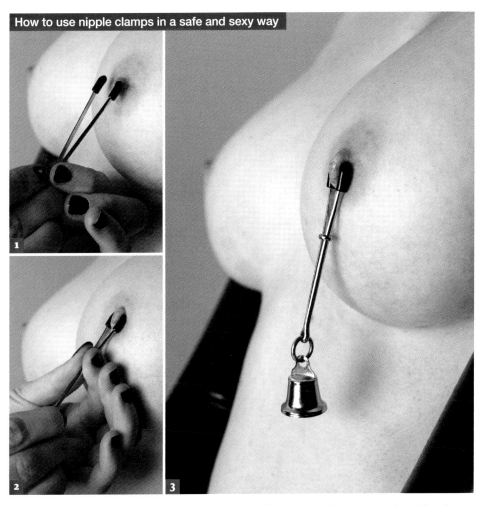

How to use nipple clamps in a safe and sexy way

1 Tweezer nipple clamps are fun and easy to put on. First open up the tweezers by sliding the ring down the shaft and opening up the end. **2** Once you have the clamp around the nipple start sliding the ring up the shaft. **3** The bells are a nice touch and will jingle as you spank, paddle and otherwise torment your slave!

for yourself and your partners, start simply and build from there. The Mona Lisa wasn't painted in a day; DaVinci worked on the painting off and on throughout his life and likely saw it as something that evolved, rather than a task to be completed. Just like DaVinci creating his Mona Lisa, it takes time and care to for us to build and trust to keep a polyamorous relationship strong as it evolves.

Open polyamory typically involves long-term couples who are open to inviting other new people to join and share in their relationship and

Pervertible tit clamps can be found at anyone's workbench.

polyfidelity tends to be closed–a relationship say between say three or four people that is not "open" to others. If you are new to polyamory, you may be surprised about the reality versus the myth that poly implies an orgy every night with multiple partners. Actually, poly concentrates on loving, emotionally and sexually centered relationships that are based on communication, integrity and honesty. As with most relationships, sex forms a loving part of it, but intimacy is the true goal of the polyamorous. Poly is not the same as swinging; we will look at the benefits and challenges of sexually open but emotionally closed relationships such as swinging later in this chapter. For most people, polyamory takes a whole lot of commitment if it's going to work long term. It requires a commitment to honesty, sexual safety, facing one's own insecurities and making difficult sacrifices when necessary. It requires standing up for yourself when it's called for, and a willingness to be with a partner through some very strong emotions. It is this activating of and moving through strong emotions that will help galvanize your relationships so that they can complement, not complicate, the lives of all involved.

Going to dinner with your unassuming vanilla friends with your butt plug in will remind you of the specialness of your kinky relationship.

Polyamory requires a great commitment to keeping an open dialog between all players. If you are going to ask someone to love and commit to you and another person, this requires being actively engaged with others' feelings, emotions and insecurities as well as your own. We are all human and jealousy will likely rear its head until you learn how to tame that beast and make it work for you, not against you. I have found that my polyamorous relationships have brought about a deeper level of honesty, self-understanding and sensitivity to my partners' feelings and desires and have resulted in a deeper intimacy than I have experienced in more traditional relationships. Others may find that involvement with more than one person takes away from the special bond or intimacy they feel being with just one. Polyamory can be a very intimate way of relating and loving, but it's certainly not the right choice for everyone. Many people wonder if there is "cheating" in poly, and there has been a lot of material published on this very subject. In my experience cheating involves deception and lying. The goal of polyamory is to encourage communication, and the openness of sharing in an emotionally loving relationship. Cheating is violating your partner's or partners' trust, whether in a poly or monogamous relationship, and that is something I do not condone.

How to Be Kinkier

Emphasizing masculine and feminine traits can heighten any mood regardless of your gender.

Being New

Perhaps you have thought about polyamory and you feel you have the right level of understanding, along with a deep commitment with someone you love, and you both are ready to take the next step and begin exploring with others. Love is all about giving. It always has been. You don't get involved with someone emotionally because you want to "get" something, you become involved because you adore that person and want to support him and help bring a light to his life. Let me say that again: Love is about giving. Let me reassure you that when you first start on this path, you will be nervous. Moving from monogamy to non-monogamy or poly is a step that isn't intuitive for most of us raised in the Western tradition where serial monogamy is the norm or standard. Use nervousness to your advantage to set the pace. Going slow is a very good way to start, and by not rushing things, you can take the time to explore at a pace that is suitable instead of jumping in feet first with your eyes closed. Take the time to work out the details and boundaries of including new people in your relationships. Be brutally honest with yourself about what you want and how you will react to what your partner wants. Glossing over important details or boundaries will jeopardize any chance poly has of working. You have to be considerate of your main partner's feelings and emotions. It isn't just about you. Multiple people require multiple considerations. People new to polyamorous relationships have to work through societal conditioning that bases its structure (in the Western world anyway) on dichotomy–the pairing of two people, sometimes monogamous, sometimes not, and the "standard" model we have of that isn't always very successful. This is where I feel poly has a really strong chance of succeeding when other models of non-monogamy don't.

Timing Is Everything

A relationship with just one other person can be a juggling act at times, and when you introduce others it can be tough, just from a time management angle. Obligations such as your job, children or charity work can put a lot of demands on your time; how can you carry on a relationship with

Facing Page: The sound of a well-made paddle hitting a gorgeous ass is always a huge turn on.

If moving to a new apartment, choose an end unit to save your neighbours from the noise you are going to make during kinky sex.

more than one person on top of all the obligations you already have? If you are going to work on incorporating polyamory into your life, you will definitely need an iPhone, BlackBerry or other smartphone with a scheduling app. Time management is one of the most valuable skills you can develop when exploring this side of yourself. Figuring out what you truly want from your partners and being able to prioritize those people and activities will force you to sharpen your planning skills. Showing up for your date on time tells someone that you not only respect her but you respect her time as well. Blowing her off because something "better" comes up is disrespectful. Sometimes you will have to make difficult choices about how and with whom you spend your time. No one wants to hurt someone's feelings because "My slave and I are going to dinner," and this is where simple etiquette and manners come into play. If you have a date with one person all set up and then bail for another, "better" offer that comes along, you are telling that other person that her time isn't nearly as important as another's and that is hurtful. If you don't have time to spend with someone who is engaging and valuable, then don't make the date in the first place. We can't always spend all the time we wish with others. Careful planning and knowing your own limitations will communicate to others that their time is valuable and treasured by you.

Where Does It Fit in BDSM?

There are a multitude of challenges to polyamory when it is framed in a BDSM context, and for this reason there are questions that you should be asking yourselves and discussing together long before they become issues. For example, what if you are collared to a Master that you have pledged your undying obedience to, and he decides to add a second slave to the household, much to your surprise? What if the Mistress decides that you are both poly now and you are going to have to learn to live with it whether or not you are comfortable with it? How will you deal with someone else vying for her attention? Did you give your undying devotion to him only to recant when it became inconvenient or uncomfortable? What if you are a Mistress who desires to cuckold her husband and then learns that he is uncomfortable with being made to wear a chastity device and sit in the corner while his wife takes another lover to their bed? What if your own values develop in such a way that you are not the same person as when you

How to do firecupping

1 First you will need a lovely and willing victim! 2 And you will need the following: 1. 70% or higher isopropyl alcohol. I prefer 91% because there is less water content and when the spark is applied there is less chance of burning from the steam that is created when the water vaporizes. 2. Fire cups of various sizes—you can typically find them in larger cities' Chinatown sections and they are quite inexpensive. The larger the cup the greater the suction 3. BBQ lighter OR locking forceps with cotton balls. I like a BBQ lighter because there is less fussing to get the flame going. 4. A candle if you are using the forceps with cotton ball method to hold the flame. 5. Eye dropper and a small dish. It is important to keep the small dish of alcohol away from where the action is. Plus a damp towel on hand is ideal for safety if you need to smother the flame.

3 First, make sure your victim doesn't have any lotion on their body. Before playing, tell them that after they bathe they shouldn't apply any creams, lotions or perfumes to their body. Pour out a small amount of isopropyl alcohol into a dish—a very small amount. This is so that your larger bottle doesn't evaporate while leaving the cap off. Close the bottle and put it aside. You don't need more than two capfuls at a time in the dish. Take the eyedropper and drip 2 drops into the fire cup. Turn the cup slightly sideways and apply the flame; it should catch fire, and hold it for a few seconds. A few seconds is all you need. Note: if you find that your flame is blowing itself out with a soft "poof" sound, you are using too much alcohol. The difference between 2 and 3 drops can be too much can be huge depending on the size of the cup. Some people like to wipe the inside of the fire cup with an alcohol swab but I find that 1 or 2 drops in the bottom is sufficient. 4 As soon as the fire catches, you want to quickly place the cup face down on the skin. The flame will eliminate the oxygen from the cup but only for a moment, you have to be quick but don't rush so much you stumble. Smooth, firm and confident movements are going to make you a sexy superstar. 5 While these images demonstrate in a step by step manner how to do this activity, and with safety foremost in our minds, they are in no way substitutes for actual hands on learning. Fire is dangerous play and you should find someone experienced in real life that can show you in person the safest way possible for you to engage in these activities. These pictures represent what is possible, after you have become proficient.

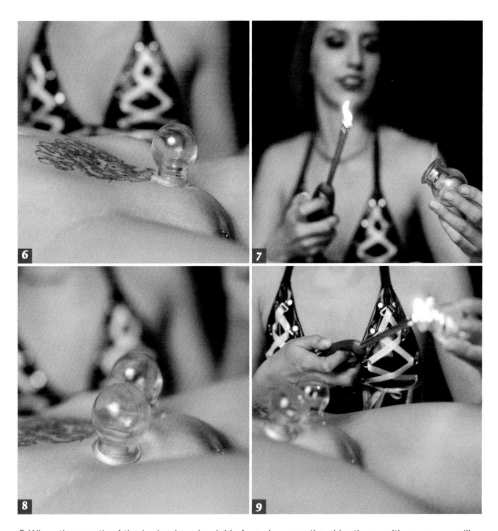

6 When the mouth of the jar is placed quickly face down on the skin, the resulting vacuum will suck the submissive's skin up and into the jar, forming a tight seal. If it isn't stuck firmly, then you weren't fast enough with plopping it down on the skin. Don't wait for the fire to burn itself out before placing it on the skin; it will extinguish itself when the seal is tight. Sure it is a bit scary but scary is fun as long as you have a real life person to walk you through this until you gain proficiency and confidence. 7 Then you can start adding more cups! As you can see in this picture, the flame is strong and blue and our top, Bri, is about to push it down on the skin quickly... 8 Get it to look like this—it has a nice tight seal. (That's what SHE said!) Playing with cups all over the area is fun and exciting. You want to look for the less boney areas—don't try doing it on a hipbone, it will fall off and break on the floor. 9 Soft, fleshy areas of the body are perfect, and as your bottom gets used to the sensation you can work towards more sensitive— and more fun!—areas of her body.

10 Yum, more cups please! The cups can be left on while the skin turns red inside it. Let the cups sit there, slowly sucking on your submissive. Let it torment them in a fun way. If done right, the submissive will have some lovely bruises for a few days after the scene.

11 For the larger areas such as the belly, back and thighs, you can start using the larger fire cups. You still only need 1-2 drops of isopropyl alcohol to light up the cup. 12 A strong blue flame is ideal. 13 Have fun with fire cupping. The longer you leave them on, the more torture it will be for the submissive. When it is time to remove it, hold the cup firmly and push down with your finger along the edge to break the vacuum seal. Don't massage or rub the area, as the submissive's body will readjust as the marks form.

Don't forget to put the *Do Not Disturb* sign on your door when staying in a hotel. Or you might suddenly make a new friend. Or two.

began a relationship? These are important issues that will arise and the best way to resolve them is by making your expectations known in the very beginning. What does your polyamorous relationship look like to you, and to your partner? In a Leather family or BDSM dynamic it is no different. Discussion has to happen long before the decisions are made. That said, polyamory can bring a lot to your kinky relationship where there is a strong emphasis on a power dynamic based on a hierarchy. This can be beneficial for the new person invited into the relationship who is being exposed to more experienced partners. Being new, it is okay to ask questions and make it clear that you are still learning. The more experienced people in the relationship have all been where you are and typically will be happy to help you along your learning curve. Joining a couple or a triad or a leather family, you will find there is the opportunity to taste many experiences with a support system well in place. The newcomer can not only expand his or her boundaries but can integrate the polyamorous model and understand it by having others to discuss it with. Having someone more experienced to say, "I understand you might be apprehensive and that is okay, but if you would like to try this activity I will go slow and you can use your safeword at any time. Plus our other partner(s) will be here to help you through it," can provide you with a sense of security: everyone involved has a role to play when a new activity is introduced in playtime. It is very reassuring to have someone there to (literally) hold your hand the first time a Dominant introduces a new sensation that might push your comfort level.

My preference for exploring polyamory shifted quickly from more traditional social relationships during a brief relationship with an open-minded, younger girlfriend. She spoke matter-of-factly about her own polyamorous nature and a desire to explore a budding interest in Leather kink with a dominant and submissive dynamic. Fear and attraction, the true power couple, kept me curious, turned on and scared. Bit by bit the foundation of what I had come to know about healthy relationships and sexuality as informed by the psychotherapeutic and second wave feminist models was crumbling. I was coming out a second time–first as a dyke at thirty-five and again to kink and

Facing Page: The Sybian can be used to tease your slave—and also to give her forced orgasms that she won't forget.

A well-placed zipper can open up a whole world of possibilities.

Water play can bring about some very strong feelings for both sub and dom.

polyamory at forty-five. While topping or observing play, I was able to see how kink and poly can intersect in a variety of ways for couples and single players. I became less afraid of poly knowing that I could control where, when and in what context I experienced it.
—Selina, Dominant

As a Dominant, I have found that utilizing the structure inherent in a BDSM–based power relationship can facilitate polyamory more easily than other models. Kinky people have a long history of discussing and communicating about issues and activities and then framing them into a hierarchy of expectations and duties. In my first poly relationship, I was with a partner who was a Switch, and we invited a submissive to join us. We had no resources to draw on, no support groups, and it was up to me as the Dominant to figure out how to keep both of them satisfied and happy with the arrangement, while still being fair and having my own needs and desires met. After a few bumps and bruises along the learning curve, we discovered that writing out clear expectations in a submissive contract between myself and her smoothed out the problems we were having, since

Choosing the outfit you want your submissive or bottom to wear before a big fetish party will make him or her feel happily controlled.

there were very specific expectations outlined. Submissives deal very well with structure–create it and use it to help them feel secure in their place.

Open Relationships and Swinging: Casual Partners Versus Primary Partner

This is an area that can work one of two ways: really well or really poorly. There isn't a lot of middle ground. This is a characteristic of all these different types of relationships and can be a great opportunity for everyone involved to stay on track with physical and emotional feelings.

Something that will become an issue for your poly relationship is learning to juggle all of your partners' needs and wants. We become involved with people for the joy and love they bring to our lives and they deserve to spend time with us that is nurturing and respectful. When we introduce a new partner into a poly relationship, we still need to be conscious of continually nurturing the other relationships we are involved in. New partners can be exciting and fun and it is easy to get lost in the thrill of a new partner but all of your other partners are very important and you don't want to jeopardize those relationships just because of a new shiny toy. I always say, *like your play, but love your partner.* You might have a partner who really likes something specific that you aren't into or can't provide; for people in open relationships, play is just "play" without emotional entanglement. The partner you have nurtured longest is a very important person in your life and there is a reason you have chosen to be with that individual: he or she has qualities that you adore and desire so much that you want to be in a relationship with them. Once you have set boundaries that you are both comfortable with, any exploration outside that relationship needs to honor those boundaries for the health of the relationship. When I play privately with new people, I like to include my other partner so that we can both share the experience. There is something delicious about sharing another partner with the person you love. Using the extra person as a complement to your playtime can be wonderful, provided that everyone is on board. Playing together with a new person is not the time to push your primary partner's boundaries. You have to have the talk about boundaries long before all of you wind up in the dungeon together. Sometimes in the heat of the moment people can get carried away, but I caution you to not let that be an excuse for selfish behavior. You can't say, "Sorry, but that was so hot

Speculums can be sexy!.

I couldn't help myself." That would be a clear indication that you can't respect boundaries and if you can't, then perhaps you shouldn't be playing with kinky sex. We want to honor and trust our partners and trust is a vulnerable thing that can be lost in a heartbeat.

When I play one on one with a new partner, I reassure my primary partner that I love and care about her and that nothing is going to get in the way of our emotional relationship. People in open relationships tend to

Don't just get stuck inside—try rope bondage in lots of different places.

gravitate toward the swinging community more than closed poly people do. I have noticed that the swinging community and the kinky community are enjoying much more cross-pollination than ever before. As little as ten years ago they seemed to be polar opposites, with the kink community not interested in swapping or sharing partners. Over time, though, more and more of the sexually adventurous have crossed back and forth, building bridges out of sexual hedonism. Swinging relationships tend to be based on sexualized encounters without the emotional connection, and that can work out well for BDSM kinksters where a couple might be emotionally monogamous but sexually open. I like to think that lately the swinging scene has helped the BDSM crowd loosen up a bit and the BDSM crowd has helped the people in the swinging scene define boundaries and limit more. In one camp you have a group devoted to hedonism and in the other, control is the priority. This exchange of ideas about how we do things has been great in making people more thoughtful about their actions.

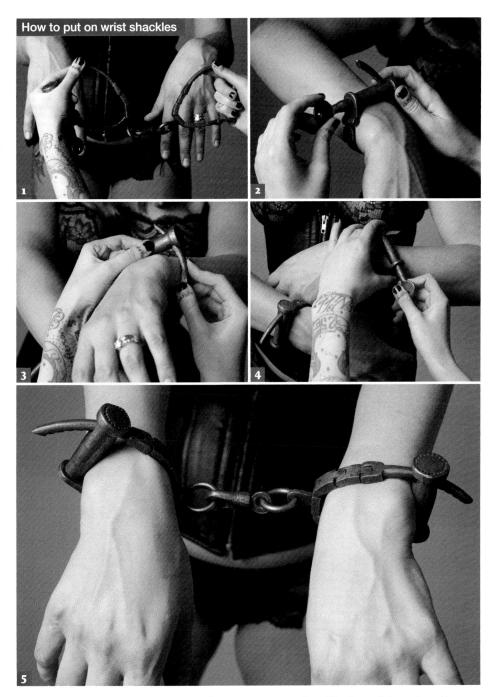

How to put on wrist shackles

1 Shackles should be the right size. 2 This style uses a turn key. Slip the end through and turn the key counter clockwise. 3 Put the turn key in and turn it clockwise to release the shackle end and fasten it about the wrist. 4 Turn the key counter clockwise to remove it end and fasten it about the wrist. 5 Voila! one captured slave.

Fantasy can enhance reality but it isn't a replacement.

Emotional Ties That Bind

In all of these relationships, and especially with poly, you are going to be dealing with multilayered dynamics. Let's look at the issue of emotional safety in poly and open relationships, which have some crossover. If you are a swinger and also feel that any of this discussion of emotional issues has applications to your life and relationships, take from it what you like! In any relationship involving more than one other person, it can be tricky at times to keep everyone on the same page and at some point someone is going to feel hurt or slighted.

The most obvious issue is jealousy. Can people in poly and open relationships experience jealousy? Of course we can. Jealousy is a natural reaction that we have when we feel threatened or insecure. It can be a powerful emotion that arises from many different situations, not just in a poly relationship. In this chapter I am going to focus on jealousy that is situation-specific. Someone might have a very low jealous nature or none in a particular situation and then suddenly have it flare up in a situation outside the norm.

I have a pair of lovely friends who are poly and who both have lovers outside their relationship. They manage their time well, making room for the other loves in their lives, but they try to share certain acts with each other that they don't with their other partners. One of their special activities is ice-skating together. Hang on…ice-skating? Why the heck am I talking about something as vanilla as ice-skating in a book on how to be kinkier? How does ice-skating relate to any of this? Stay with me for a moment while I explain. As children growing up at either end of the country they enjoyed figure skating and playing hockey with the people close to them–family and close friends. They had such fond memories of it that when they met and fell for each other they realized that they both shared a love and passion for the activity and it dovetailed beautifully with their attraction to each other. It was something that connected them on an emotional and physical level. It was one of those special activities that we share with our partners when we date and spend time together–it could be bowling, discussing books or fisting each other on a Friday night at the local pansexual bar. Then one weekend one of them couldn't make their ice-skating date and without considering much about the situation the other partner, who still wanted to go, invited her other lover along because she felt it was a fun activity she would like to share with someone close to her.

Can there be anything more gorgeously helpless than a sub in a gimp mask and leg spreader bars?

The more perverted the mind, the better the toys!

When the first partner found out, he was confronted with feelings of jealousy, as in "How can she go skating without me–that was for us!" He felt hurt and left out. Insecurity and jealousy welled up inside him and he was having a hard time processing those feelings. Neither of them had ever talked about going ice-skating with others; perhaps they thought it might never come up or they each assumed that they were both saving it as an activity just for them.

So what did he do? He investigated his jealousy and took a hard look at the feelings he was having, investigating his own boundaries, and he mastered them. They talked together about the kind of reaction he was having to this seemingly innocent activity. She was surprised and shocked and very sympathetic and he communicated what ice-skating with her meant to him. They clarified their feelings and decided that since that activity meant so much to him and connected him to her so deeply, emotionally, they would either do it just with each other or when the other was present, one of them might bring along another partner so that everyone could enjoy it together as a group.

Here's a personal example from a little closer to the dungeon floor: I was at a Kink Conference and was having my boots polished and tended to by the local bootblack. Afterwards this hunky bear asked if he could give my boots a good licking and I love boot licking so I ordered him to his knees and let him go to town. Little did I know that the new primary relationship I was nurturing was with a woman who loved to lick my boots but had never communicated to me how deeply intimate it was for her. When she found out I had been "slutting my boots around," she was very upset because it meant so much to her on an intimate level. I listened to her, took what she had to say to heart and made her feel that she had really been heard and that in order to safeguard against this reaction happening again, we both needed to work on more open communication so we would know what was expected from us. These models of how to successfully deal with feelings that arise don't always have sex at the root: here, the issue was intimacy.

Jealousy isn't something to fear as an emotion, it is something to master if you are going to be in a poly relationship. It is a strong emotion and you have to take a hard look at yourself and your own needs and expectations and communicate those with your partners, who should support you as you work through those feelings. What I love about my poly friends is the

Gag him with your panties. Bonus if he can taste you.

109

Some daily rituals can be applied in vanilla settings to keep the mindset going.

way they openly discuss feelings that may stay buried in other more conventional relationships. They seek out those feelings that are causing distress and they talk about them and work through them together. Your polyamorous relationships should be there to support and nurture you on your journey through life, not detract from your experience. Poly people see jealousy as a warning sign that there is some uncovered issue that isn't resolved. They want to uncover those issues, talk about them, examine the root of the feeling and attempt to overcome it. What winds up happening is that the more jealousy arises in a poly relationship and is dealt with successfully, the easier it becomes to work through.

This is all well and good and a little hippy dippy with the feelings, but what are some concrete steps you can take if there is some distress occurring in the relationship? What do you do if you are the cause of someone else's distress? How will you validate your partner's feelings and smooth things out if you are indeed the one at fault? Conflict is going to happen more often than not, and we deal with it as adults, not by throwing a hissy fit. What follows are some constructive ideas on how to deal with missteps and hurt feelings so that the other person can feel heard and reassured that you are apologizing for the right thing instead of just using a blanket apology without investigating whether or not you are at the root of the problem. The worst thing you can do is apologize for something that you are not to blame for. There are three simple rules to frame your reaction and help you on the way to mending things if you are the cause:

■ Identify the root of the problem and figure out who is at fault.

■ Validate the other person's feelings.

■ Apologize and mean it and then make sure it doesn't happen again.

Sounds simple, doesn't it? Amazingly, some people act like babies whenever confronted with criticism, or when they encounter friction in their love lives, but being involved in polyamorous relationships requires that you pay careful attention to other partners' feelings. If you care about each other you will work through the bumps that will arise as you all evolve in your relationships. Above all else, ask them what they need. You don't have to try to guess; communication is a two-way street. If the other person is misguided in his blame, figure out together what is the real issue and if you are to blame, take responsibility for it. If not, encourage

Facing Page: The more dramatic your dress up, the hotter your scene.

Carry multiple handcuff keys— even on your car key ring.

the other person to take a hard look at her reactions and where they might be coming from. Taking the time to discuss the problem itself without initially laying blame is an important first step and a mature act; it means that you are actively communicating. If, after you discuss the problem, you conclude that you are not to blame, don't apologize and certainly don't apologize for someone else's feelings. You can only own your own actions and emotions. Being responsible enough to fix the problem you caused is going to reveal and strengthen your character, not detract from it. If the problem is your fault, treat it as a learning opportunity so that you don't repeat the same mistake twice; once is a mistake, twice is just stupid. Compassion and kindness go a long way in any relationship, not just poly and open ones.

Safe Sex Is Sexy

What are the risks you are willing to take? Do you play only with condoms and dental dams? Do you use birth control? Do you know your partner intimately and understand who they will be with and what that person's sexual life involves? Safer sex is very sexy to others and if you are known for playing safe, you will find potential partners more attracted to you. My number one rule of safety at all times is Know Your Partners. There should never be a situation where someone says, "Oh, I don't what his health status is; I never bothered to ask." If you are going to be with multiple partners then I suggest the buddy system. Just like when you were in swim class as a child–you looked out for your buddy and he looked out for you. In poly and open relationships, you will have multiple buddies, not just one. Check in with them, find out what is going on and get tested on a regular basis. Having regular open communication about who you are seeing and when and what activities might be involved or what you did last weekend will make any conversation that involves a heavier subject easier to talk about if at some point your sexual health is compromised. You have other partners and their sexual health to think about, not just your own. Don't be selfish; be open and discuss these issues before you play. If your reputation is one of being a safe partner who takes time and care regarding safe sex then your attractiveness in the community will go upward. If you have a terrible reputation for being selfish and self-centered with your emotional and physical safety, you aren't going to find many people willing to

Be creative with your microbondage and yarn. The pool is a great place to practice since they can't hurt themselves if they fall over.

be with you. I always find it interesting that vanilla people don't tend to be subject to this type of social circle warning system. It's one of the checks and balances that help our communities police themselves.

Questions I ask myself before I get involved with new play partners: Do they practice safe sex? What are their other partners' practices like? How

In the right hands, a simple paddle is one of the best toys there is.

comfortable are they with discussing health issues with their physician? How often do they have STI testing and can they show me the results when I show them mine? What are their limits with kinky play, e.g., whipping, bondage, blood play, et cetera, and how do they dovetail with my own interests or limits? In a casual play setting do they need aftercare, and can I provide it or not?

A vibrating toothbrush is the perfect traveling companion. Plus it is waterproof!

Your sexual health is important and you should cherish it, not subject it to unnecessary risks. Kinkier play and situations are fun and awesome, but you need to make positive, healthy sexual choices and only you can be responsible for that.

By choosing an open or closed poly or an open relationship, you are opening yourself up to more than one partner on emotional, mental *and* physical levels. Discussing what is intimate and meaningful to you and your partners and establishing clear boundaries will help you all to nurture your relationships and have fun exploring others and welcoming them. Your sexual health and safety is important; there is nothing more expensive than regret. In chapter 7 we will look in more detail at ways we can play safely with others.

Five Key Points for Poly and Open Relationships:

■ Communicate, communicate, communicate

■ It is okay to feel jealous at times; use the emotion for personal growth so you can master it

■ When making an apology, make it sincere

■ Poly doesn't always mean open, and open doesn't always mean poly

■ Poly can work very well in a BDSM hierarchy with a specific structure

Chapter Five

Advanced Sex Toys and How to Use Them

There are toys for all ages.
—French Proverb

One of the reasons I love kinky sex so much is all the fun and creative toys it comes with! As mentioned earlier, I keep my toys in my grandmother's old hope chest, and even now it is overflowing. Granny would be spinning in her grave if she knew what I was using it for, but I can't help it—it is a beautiful cedar-lined walnut chest from the 1930s, and I have a *lot* of toys. If you are new to collecting toys, let me describe the pattern of your near future: it all starts with putting a few toys in a drawer in the bedside stand, then, as you add a paddle or two, a dildo here, a butt plug there, some cuffs and rope— the toy collection grows to two drawers, then the whole nightstand, and the next thing you know you are pushing your shoe collection over to the side in the closet to make room for your handmade floggers and cane collection. Toy collections grow and grow; believe me, this is going to happen to you; it cannot be helped. Extra bonus points if you can hide the collection successfully where there are children in the house. If you think their snooping for Christmas presents is bad, imagine yourself trying to explain the strap-on harness

Facing Page: When you zap them, they will want to jump around. Make sure you have a hold of them.

with the ten-inch black silicone cock that "daddy likes when he's feeling pretty" that they found because you didn't lock your toy box.

There is such a myriad of toys, both store-bought and handmade: you can plug, hit, mark, scratch, tickle or torture someone with thousands of items—some made cheaply, some pervertible ones (household items adapted from their conventional use), and still others crafted by skillful artisans. This chapter focuses on some of my favorite "kinkier" toys, how to apply them in new and creative ways, and how best to travel with them. First, let's talk about quality, and why supporting your local and national artisans is important. In *How to Be Kinky*, I wrote about the need for us to support those people who handcraft their kinky wares out of the love they have for kinky play, rather than buy cheap toys that are mass produced, and the value of our getting to know the Murphy whip makers of today who will be held in the highest regard for their craft down the road. There are lots of kinky craft fairs nowadays around North America (Google is your best friend for tracking these down) and you have many opportunities to buy from the people who don't do it to become rich but because they love it. Larger companies that I buy locally from and would recommend are Northbound and Aslan Leather, For Your Nymphomation toy cases or Ego Assassin and Kink Engineering Latex. That much said, cheap, disposable and mass-produced toys also have their place in the kink scene—just recognize that a cheap toy is ultimately the more expensive one because when it breaks you have to buy another and throw out the old one. Some toys that hold the fondest memories for me are a pair of floggers crafted by a wonderful woman back in the 1990s. The braiding is tight on the handle; her Turk's head knots are perfect, and the tails of the floggers are made of the highest quality leather. These floggers look and perform just as well today and maybe even better than the day I purchased them. The price I paid for them divided over fifteen years of play is such a small amount for such a high-quality pair of floggers. I have since found another flogger maker—Master Andre out of Montreal—whose work is just as exceptional, and I have been buying from him and his wife for several years now. If you fall in love with something handmade by an artisan, don't hesitate to buy it and brighten your life, because you never know how long the artisan will be in business. The more we support kinky artisans, the

For a sensual connection during a scene try to maintain three points of contact and match your partner's breath on the inhale and exhale.

Facing Page: Who needs a boring vibrator when you can have a steampunk vibrator gun?

Dry-erase marker
washes off easily.

more time they can dedicate to the evolution of their craft. I make an active choice to support businesses that are working hard to create new and interesting toys of high quality, and I encourage you to do the same. Now that my toy collection has grown out of control, I have a rule that I follow when I'm on the road that slows down the acquisition of new items but keeps the collection of a high quality. I only buy a toy if: 1) I have never seen it before, or 2) I probably will never see it again, and 3) the price is right. This rule works for the most part but there have been decisions I regret. I still kick myself for not picking up a super swanky Austrian glass dildo with feathers delicately attached with a jeweled strap to the handle; the eight-hundred-plus price tag prohibited me from picking it up. I *really* wanted it, and I still do, but you have to have boundaries when buying toys, otherwise you will go broke pretty fast. Kinky sex is about respecting boundaries sometimes, even if we don't like them; especially if that boundary comes with an 18 percent interest rate on your credit card.

Creative Adaptation: Pervertibles

So what happens if you aren't able to bring your favorite floggers on the road with you? Rest assured there are the "pervertibles"—everyday objects "perverted" from their intended vanilla use and turned into creative toys. The only limit is the boundary of your own creativity. How twisted are you? What do you want to get out of a scene or playtime with a partner? Where do you want to take them or be taken? Rubber gloves, a hairbrush, twenty inches of athletic wrap and a jar of strawberry jam can open up endless possibilities for a night of fun with your play partner in a cheap hotel. Ever tie your partner to the desk in a Holiday Inn, bent over with his or her ass stuck out, and when you swing your belt at his bum you almost take out the desk lamp? Yeah, me too! Well, that is a great and quick way to achieve a good spanking if you don't have your favorite readymade toys handy.

My favorite pervertible is the simple wooden kitchen spoon. There is something so classically 1950s housewife about it that has such appeal to my sense of service and belonging. My Dominant makes me clench it in my teeth and crawl to him and present it, so that I am the deliverer of my own instrument of torment. The sound is so addictive, that whoosh *through the air accompanied by the* SMACK *on my ass as the cupped side impacts and makes it extra loud while I*

This flogger has a polished aluminum handle with rubber tails, perfect for insertion and easy for cleaning up after

A fiddle is a one piece locking collar and cuff made out of metal, useful for endurance play.

kick my feet helplessly. Loud spanking sounds have always turned me on. The handle can be flipped around and used for pussy torment and for Kegel challenges. He likes to make me stand with my legs apart and then lubes up my already slick pussy and slides the handle into me and orders me to clench my pussy around it and not let it drop out or else suffer the consequences.
—Kittenlicious submissive

What I love so much about pervertibles is that they are toys you create with your own dirty little mind—and I'm sure it is pretty damn filthy if you picked up this book. Toys are merely tools and objects; the people behind them make the scene steamy hot! Toys can be fetishized, but there is something extra special about creating something out of limited resources. Being able to improvise with what you have on hand can mean the difference between playing or not playing; between creating a magnificent or a mundane night. We don't always meet people in a fetish club while we have our toy bag with us. Sometimes we don't even have our toy bags nearby: I have done scenes in clubs involving electrical extension cords, a length of garden hose and tweezers that were just as effective at bringing someone to tears as the most expensive snake whip I own.

> *From cell phones to silk scarves to emery boards and leather belts, pervertibles are being used by more and more people for a number of reasons. Some people simply don't have room in their homes to keep a St. Andrew's cross or a spanking bench, let alone a fully stocked dungeon. They're convenient when you're traveling: no major city lacks a dollar, hardware or grocery store. One place that pervertibles make a difference between a good and a great time is in role-play. The mechanic who decides to take his payment in sex because you can't afford the cost of that new transmission and begins to tie you up with his high-quality hemp bondage rope won't be as believable as the one who uses a spare set of jumper cables, will he? A kidnapping scene where your abductors come with padded leather restraints won't be as thrilling as the abductors who roughly bind your hands with duct tape and use a pillowcase as a hood. Pervertibles help set the mood and keep the scene authentic to your fantasy.*
> —Dan, the twisted teddy bear

Here are some of my favorite toys—some improvised pervertibles and some readymade:

If you played with a permanent marker, hand sanitizer does a better job than most soaps at removing it from skin.

Balloon Anal Beads

Balloon fetishists are going to love this one! Take a clown balloon and blow it up and make a knot. These types of balloons are more rugged than your regular balloons, but you still need to be careful of any sharp objects. If you build the beads according to the instructions, you will find that they are very rugged and if one layer pops, the rest will remain intact—but let's not go digging around in there with a BBQ skewer, shall we? What I love most about balloon anal beads is their disposability. With twenty to thirty minutes before a playdate you can customize the anal beads to the size you want for your partner and when you are done you can toss them in your garbage. All it takes is creativity and some dexterous fingers.

A blindfold and raspy voice can reap major benefits.

Evil Sticks

Evil Sticks are small graphite rods that cause a stinging sensation on the skin. Hit the skin hard enough and you will raise a welt. What I love about Evil Sticks is the shapes that they have at their ends. The heart shape is particularly delicious for when you want to show your lover how much you care about his or her bottom or back. Because the striking is so concentrated and will cause a rush of blood just under the surface of the skin, I like to use these on the fleshier parts of the body—the bum, the back and the thighs—when I want to mark someone up intensely but yet know that the marks will fade by the end of the evening.

Better Living with Electricity

Obviously, you should be careful when using electricity for kinky sex. You should find proper, personal instruction before attempting to use these toys. They are deliciously evil and also deliciously pleasurable in the hands of a person who is trained properly. They aren't complicated, but you do need to find someone who can train you in a hands-on environment before escalating willy-nilly to "I'm gonna zap you good!" with your partner. There are some wonderful resources and classes given by experts that will show you how to do this safely and creatively and I highly encourage you to access

Facing Page: Even the modest balloon can be perverted for dozens of sexy uses.

A trip to the hardware store with a kinky mind can be a lot of fun!

them. A good general rule of thumb is that we are not going to use electrical toys above the waist, over the heart or on the head (with the exception of the Violet wand—more on that in a moment). Keep it below the belt, which is where the good bits are anyway. Electrical toys can scare the shit out of the bottom when experienced for the first time and we all love a good mind fuck don't we? But truthfully, it's best when dealing with a newbie to let them play with the controls on their own at first, so they can experience firsthand what the sensations are and how strong they can be. Think of it as a warm-up for a dance rather than taking away from your playtime. You can make it fun, light and enjoyable by explaining what each part is, what it does, and how to control it. I find that after a little playing with the dial before the scene, and by your keeping the mood light and playful and letting them feel like they are in charge (at first), they will be dripping honeyholes by the time you are ready to begin. So what happens if they don't like it? Easy: now you know that they aren't into it and you can take your scene in a different direction. It is better to gauge their reaction before you get them all tied up in one hundred feet of rope and swinging from your ceiling. And if they say no and mean no (i.e., they use their safeword) then respect it; after all, they are the ones that were going to take that big steel plug inside them and have electrical current passed through it, not you. Don't be disappointed; smile and say, "Okay, I understand," and then keep the momentum going in a different direction and don't tease them about it. Let the submissives' curiosity bring them back to it on their own. Slow is easy and there's the potential for a serious mishap if you rush into things.

Electrical toys are divided into two types: the ones based on current (TENS units) and the ones based on voltage (cattle prods and violet wands). I am going to talk about the differences between each and you can choose which one you want to explore for use in your own kinky life.

What Nerve(s): TENS

TENS (Transcutaneous Electrical Nerve Stimulation) unit or insertable toys are electrical devices for which you can control the amount of electricity being emitted via a dial or slider that works on electrical muscle contraction—they're used mostly for recovering from athletic injuries. You can purchase them off the shelf at the drugstore and they can really add a charge to your sex life! They need to be attached to the skin over the

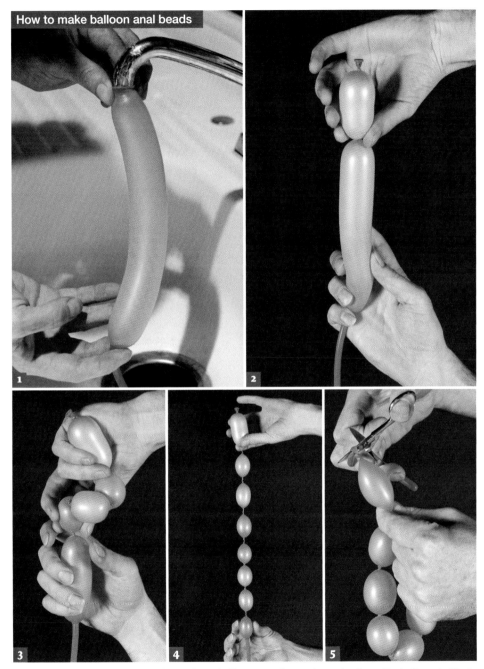

How to make balloon anal beads

1 Water filled anal beads made from circus balloons are fun and easy! 2 Once the balloon is filled with water, start twisting each bead along the length of the balloon. 3 Make as many as you like, but make sure to hang onto each one so it doesn't unwind itself as you are making them. 4 Hang on to the ends. Momentarily you won't have to, but for now, keep hold of each end. 5 Knot and snip the extra end off.

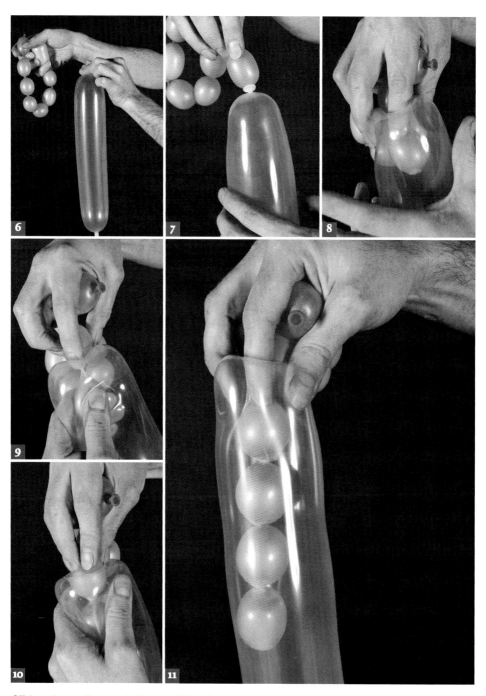

6 Take a larger diameter balloon and blow it up. 7 Knot the end and now get ready to push. 8 You are pushing the water filled balloon into the larger one; keep a good hold of everything. 9 Here is the tricky part. Once you push it inside you have to twist the larger balloon around each bead. 10 Then push the next one in. 11 You are going to gently push all of them inside the larger balloon.

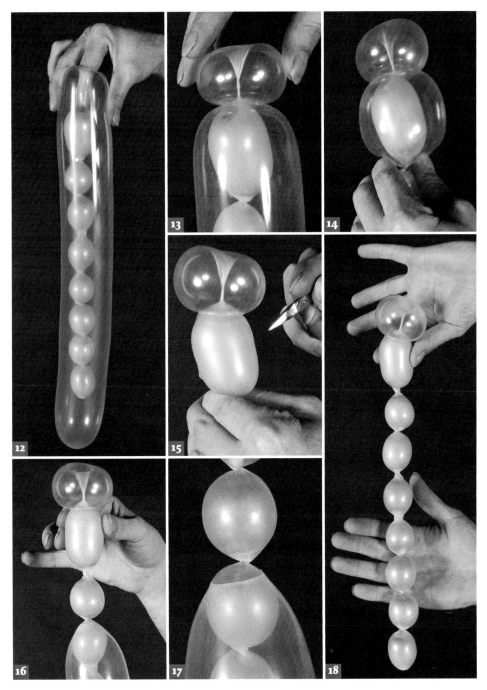

12 It should look like this. 13 Then twist the top off to seal it. 14 This part might not make sense but once you have the top part twisted off, twist off the lower part down one bead. 15 Then pop the top one. 16 Now start to slide the beads up and out. 17 This puts an extra layer on the beads. 18 It should look like this.

19 Trim off the excess. **20** Get another balloon, something with a pretty colour. **21** You are going to repeat the same steps from 7 – 17. **22** I like to choose different colours for each layer.

23 Everytime you put an extra layer on it, the stronger it will get. **24** One last layer here.

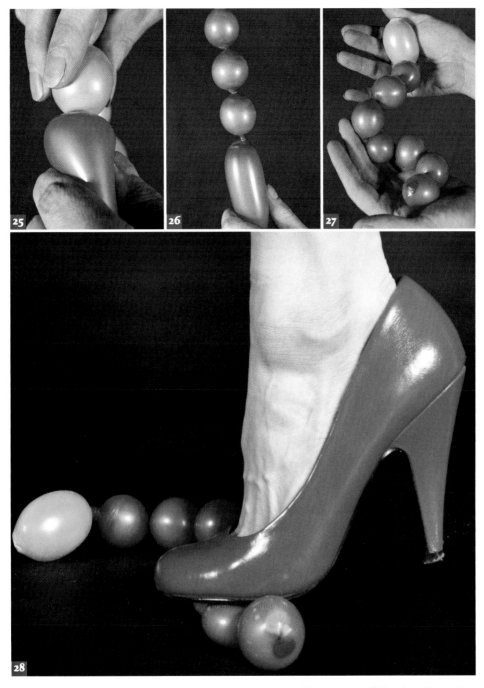

25 You will find that the beads are starting to feel stronger and firmer now. 26 The nice thing is that since they are filled with water, they give when inserting them, making it more comfortable. 27 With a few balloons for under a dollar you can make a new set of anal beads each time you play and look how pretty they are!. 28 And tough! Even if one layer pops, they will seldom all pop at once.

How to use Evil Sticks

1 Evil Sticks are small graphite rods with a slapper end in different shapes. 2 You pull it back and let it go onto the skin with a sharp wack. 3 With this heart shaped stick, the flatter the head is when it hits the skin... 4 the more success you will have in creating a heart!

The mushroom attachment on a violet wand.

top of a muscle or the beginning and end of the muscle or else they won't be particularly effective; just placing the sticky pads on the cock and balls won't do much. If you have a basic sense of anatomy and the locations of muscle groups, you can turn these tools into wonderfully evil toys. Ask yourself, "What muscles do we have below the belt?" How about the anal sphincter and the pubis? The insertable plugs such as dildos and butt plugs come in a variety of sizes and shapes. When electrodes are hooked up to the points on the plug, it causes contractions in the pelvic muscle and sphincter. You can tune the box to set up a random sequence of charges so that the pretty little submissive bound tightly to your table never knows when it is coming. Or better yet, set it for a regular interval and tell her, "It is going to shock you every twenty-five seconds. Watch the clock on the wall so you know when it is coming!" Then sit back and watch your victim sweat and fret and squirm. A nice ball gag in her mouth will add to your excitement. Stay away from Tasers and stun guns; they will not only ruin the scene, but you might wind up on the evening news. As with all kinky play, YOU are ultimately accountable for what happens, so play safe with these toys.

133

How to use a TENS unit to electrify your playtime

1 This TENS unit has 4 dials and two buttons to control the power and the channel. **2** There are different attachments you can use. This one is a electrified dildo. **3** Turn on the power to the level you desire and you can use a thin water based lube which will conduct electricity. **4** Once it is in you can control how strong the sensations are on the dildo by the depth of it inside your slave.

5 When you are ready for more fun, flip them over and get their asshole lubed up! **6** The butt plug attachment will have two metal strips down each side for conducting electricity. **7** Just like the vibrator attachment, you can fuck them in and out and the sensations are adjustable this way as well as on the box. Enjoy!

Get Along Little Doggie: Cattle Prods

These are handheld devices from farm stores that typically run on C or D-size batteries. They deliver a three-volt (the average) shock via two prongs upon contact with someone's bum. Depending on how fresh the batteries are, the sensation ranges from, "Oh, that has a bit of a zap doesn't it?" to "Motherfucker, Morph, that fucking thing feels like it is biting me!" I don't use cattle prods above the waist; I prefer to zap the large fleshy part of the bum and legs. Keep in mind these are tools that are used to coerce large farm animals: use sparingly and with caution. They provide a really great punishment or make a good prop for threatening a slave, especially if he or she is down. Don't confuse a cattle prod with a Taser or stun gun—it is a different device entirely. If you live where there are agriculture stores, cattle prods are easy to find, relatively cheap and fun!

Lexan cutting boards make great paddles.

When You Wish Upon a Star: Violet Wand

On the other end of the spectrum, the violet wand is safe to use above the waist since the electricity doesn't penetrate down into the muscle; it's all surface fun. When activated it forms a pretty purple arc from the glass attachment that will bridge to the skin, causing the recipient to jump! When you use it, keep it below the neck and away from the eyes. With older models that are sometimes sold at fetish events, avoid letting the device heat up too much, which can happen if you leave it running continuously for more than ten minutes. This isn't a problem with the newer models.

Once you know what they look like, you will start noticing violet wands at antique markets. There are some beautiful vintage ones that can be bought for a very affordable price. The nice thing about violet wands is that you can tune the intensity from a light tickle when on low to a very intense sensation when turned up high. Once I had a submissive who really loved cutting and knife play, however she couldn't go back home with marks after our dates–that was her boundary with our play. When I was still cutting my teeth back in the day and was new to violet wands, I was playing with her in a great, gritty little fetish club in a basement of a bar (the best clubs always seem to be underground, don't they?) and I figured out that we could simulate the sensation of cutting by using both the violet wand's glass in

Facing Page: A cattle prod isn't just to thrill cows.

137

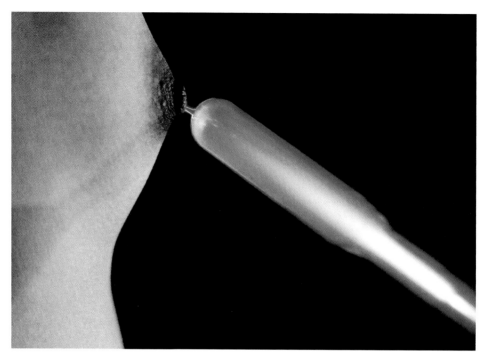

The wand can make anywhere on your body feel magical!

The juice from fresh ginger can be used to add excitement to someone's genitals.

one hand and then running a steel Whartenburg wheel across her with my other. The tiny points on the wheel allowed the electricity to flow directly through my body from the wand to the mean, tiny points on the wheel. This felt like a knife on her body, one with which she was being sliced open. Afterward she would happily go home without any marks on her skin and it was the best of both worlds! Some other fun things you can do with the violet wand are zapping your play partners on their genital piercings—some will conduct better than others—as well as varying the speed at which you drag the wand across the body. Using it in a room with the lights dimmed makes it so much cooler to look at while it is happening too.

Not So Nice: Figging

Ginger just isn't for cooking anymore. Discover what the Victorians knew: its effective merriment will put some heat in your slave's seat! Essentially figging is taking a ginger root, carving it into a butt plug shape and sticking it in your partner's bum. Ginger will produce an intense and long-lasting sensation from the juices reacting to the delicate tissues of the anus. This

The Whartenburg wheel comes with points to roll along the skin.

How to do figging

1 Figging is a fun way to spice up your submissive's anal play. 2 Get some fresh ginger from the market and break off a large finger. 3 Remove the outer skin. 4 Shape it into a butt plug. 5 Make sure it is large enough to be fun. 6 It should always have a large enough base so that you don't have a fishing trip story to tell later on!

140

7 Making the submissive watch while you shape it is a great way to make them nervous. Have them climb up on the counter... **8** and bend over. **9** Use a lot of spit or water to lubricate their butthole, as lube will dull the sensations. **10** In we go! Keep it in there as long as they can stand it.

Use lotion on the skin before using liquid latex.

is a type of heavier interaction for people who really like intense ass play or those who are very adventurous. Be forewarned that the oils that cause the burning sensation need to be processed by the body; even after you take the ginger out; you can't wash it away. If you want to start slowly, you can try a water-soluble heat like wasabi powder, which can be washed off with water if the sensation becomes too intense, and then slowly work up to ginger.

Start by cutting off a decent-sized finger from the "hand" of ginger and whittle it down into a butt plug shape. It should be three inches long with a flared base and a retention ring (see photos). The flared base is important for anything that goes in the ass so we don't lose it inside the rectum. Lay them out, restrain them and get their ass ready for a volcanic violation. Here is an interesting point—lube will dull the sensations, so if you have a newbie, you may want to keep that in mind and use some lube to tone it down a bit. To increase the sensations, don't use any lube, just some spit and water. Be very, very gentle and slow working it into the bum. Not using lube will make things more sensitive. The juices of the ginger will help lubricate it for sliding in and soon it should be socketted snuggly in their ass. The burning sensation will ramp up and become intense. If your bottom is new to figging, you can remove it and let her catch her breath. Make it as intense or mild as you like. While I haven't heard of allergies to ginger, I can't make broad sweeping generalizations for the general populace; it pays to know all about the bum you are sticking the plug into, so ask. Figging appeals to a lot of people who also enjoy the sensation of menthol on their privates; for some it is a big turn-on, for others it is a way to spice up their sex life a bit. If you are feeling sadistic, spanking or caning an ass that has ginger in it will make the sensations more intense and they won't be able to clench their cheeks together to withstand the blows. It is deliciously evil. And not only is ginger available at any grocer's, the fact that you can whip up a nice ginger stir fry after a figging session and serve it to the submissive whose bum you have just violated makes it top notch in my little black book of evil tricks.

A Laughing Matter: Tickling

I am including tickling here in the toys section because it is a wonderful overall use of toys, and if you get caught at a fetish party without your toy bag, you can use your fingers or some simple props like a feather or long

Tickling your submissive while suspended is extra special torment.

piece of faux fur. Also pervertibles such as a comb or ballpoint pen can easily be turned into a delicious, devilish device! The object is secondary to the use of it, and I highly encourage you to explore alternatives. Tickling can bring up a host of different reactions. Explaining why people are enthralled by this fetish is pretty uncomplicated—D/s, helplessness, forced reactions, humiliation; the fact that no matter how stubborn a slave may be, nobody can evade the talented fingers of an experienced tickler. There can be a lot of laughter with tickling even as you are driving them to the edge: we call it play for a reason!

There are so many ways to tickle torture submissives and just as many spots on their bodies to access, all while keeping them helpless. Here are some of my secrets for making a tickling scene fun, playful and torturous. The best method is to tie your victim into position so that you can get at

Mounting rings to the underside of a bed frame can provide handy and hidden tie-down points.

143

You can be creative with what you tickle your partner with.

Wooden toys give really mean marks when you get spanked with them.

the sweet spots. There is the classic spread-eagle position with them on their back; the "inverse Y" where their legs are tied apart with their arms tied straight above their head; the hog-tie; and them on their back with their legs tied up in the air with their wedding tackle exposed. The position can have a significant impact on their ticklishness, and it can vary from day to day or scene to scene. What worked 100 percent one day may not be as effective the next time you play. All the more reason to keep a tickling scene fresh and interesting with different positions and items to tickle them with! When bottoms are unable to see or anticipate the tickling attack, they usually scream and beg frantically. It is a great way to mind-fuck them. For myself, I love to aim at the area along the high sides of their ribs, right beside their nipples. Trailing a feather languidly and slowly, inch by delicious inch; seeing their tummy flex and squirm, their arms tugging at their bonds, their breathing coming in shallow pants; watching their squirming to shift mere inches to avoid your efforts but they simply cannot get away from it: that is a spot so sensitive and sweet you would have to be Mrs. Butterworth to be sweeter. I have found the following sweet spots to be the best:

High inner thigh: This spot is a winner. The submissives I tickle go

Rope bondage is aesthetically pleasing as well as very sexy.

absolutely insane when tickled on the inner thighs right beside the perineum, that area between the vagina and anus (or, if your victim is a man, just under the ball sack and before his anus). The trick is to keep the tickles moving between the area over the vagina and back to the inner thigh.

Hips: This is another great spot that reacts well to more "pointy" objects as well as soft. Poking lightly with both thumbs on the bone can be incredibly torturous for your poor tickle slave. Light tickles can work equally well; you can have a really wide range of reactions to different objects here.

Feet: The all-time classic spot! Here is my super duper secret tip—lube up their feet with water-based lube and then let it dry. Dried lube increases the ticking sensations by two times! This is a great entry level tickle spot and you can lure newbie partners into it by offering them a foot massage and lulling them into a nice dreamy headspace before you unleash your evil machinations on their tender tootsies. If your slave is already good with foot tickling, try putting them into a hog-tie. Face down does wonders for inhibiting the brain's capability to predict ticklish sensations, and being tied like this contributes to their helplessness. Dragging a long sharp nail down the sole of the foot while your victim is tied this way is one of

Colorful soft cotton rope is cheap at any magic supply store.

Floggers can be used for soft caressing as well as heaving beating. Mix it up.

the most beautiful tickling tortures you can put your submissive through.

I like to keep a tickling scene varied and fresh each time I do it. Sometimes I will tie the bottom's toes together with some yarn or pretty ribbon—bottoms love to be "all prettied up"—and then I use lube to slick up their feet. Then I use a sharper object like a comb or ballpoint pen and drag it across their skin. Interestingly, tying someone so that they are completely helpless isn't always better. I have seen playdates where a submissive is more frantic and helpless if he is tickled while not tied up. Plus you get to chase him or her across the bed and yank her back into position if she gets too far. Or better yet, ORDER your submissive to "Get your ass back over here; I am not done with you yet!" and then watch that internal struggle of desire and regret fight inside behind her eyes. If you are going to tie with a minimal amount of rope, give them a little slack so they think they can almost get away but in reality they *can't*; that is immensely frustrating and entertaining.

Remember: mood is everything. Create a playful atmosphere where he or she feels safe and you will have one big gooey puddle of submissive on your hands when you are through. Ultimately, tickling is fascinating and your slave will either love it or hate it. Take the time to introduce it properly and be open to learning new things. If you are into heavy play in your kinky life, try doing the harder pain activities first, before you move into tickling. Not only does it provoke quite the mind fuck, but sensitivity after pain always increases. It is a great compliment to the scene in the dungeon and will give you a wider range of activities to draw from to make your play even steamier!

Traveling with Sex Toys

Sooner or later you are going to hit the road and you will undoubtedly want to bring some of your toys with you. There is something hot and dirty about meeting up in a cheap hotel for a kinky rendezvous for thirty-six hours. Of course you will want to have your favorite playthings with you. However, as we all know, air travel both domestically and internationally has changed significantly since 2001. If the Transport Security Authority (TSA) gets all humpy over you bringing shampoo in your carry-on, you

Facing Page: Pulling hair is a classic way to make your submissives behave.

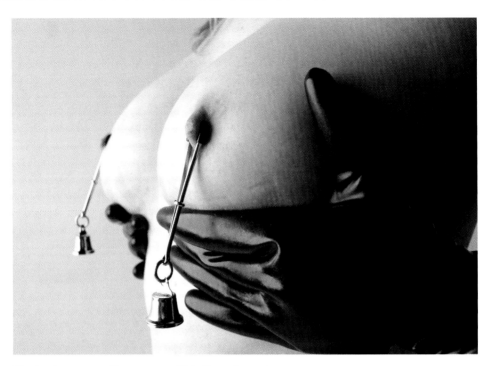

Nipple clamps sometimes come with bells on the ends.

can bet your electrical stimulation equipment is going to do more than raise a few eyebrows. If they let you make your plane, they will certainly be keeping it if you try to bring it in your carry-on luggage. You *can* travel with your toys, but you need to use some common sense, pay attention to the rules and regulations regarding restricted and prohibited items and put all your stuff in your checked luggage. If it looks like it could be a weapon (floggers, whips or zappy things like Tasers) don't even think of trying to bring it in your carry-on bags. You might be emotionally attached to a gorgeous flogger you have owned for years but the TSA doesn't care about how much you love it; they will be happy to confiscate it and toss it in a bin for disposal and you will lose it forever. When I travel I tend to take toys or items that, if push came to shove and they were confiscated., I wouldn't miss all that much. My luxurious handmade hemp and jute rope stays at home, and I take some solid and effective hemp rope for bondage with me. Likewise for other toys: in my personal collection I have a unique and eclectic selection of toys that are unusual and rare. These are not toys I would want to give up to the airport security people, so I leave my AAA-grade bird's-eye maple paddle at home. Same goes for the one made out of alligator hide or my E-Stim electrical toys.

Other toys that have sentimental value, like my lovingly braided chain leash or the big scary hunting knife I have owned since I was thirteen, all stay in my toy chest at home. While you're on the road, your toys are going to be well used, and remember that your luggage is going to be thrown around by a ramp guy whose main interest is how fast he can get it into the belly of the plane to shorten the plane's turnaround time. Don't be upset because you simply *had* to bring that three-hundred-dollar glass dildo along on a business trip and by the time you open up your luggage at the hotel it's been broken into three pieces; it's your fault for bringing it. This isn't to say we can't bring any of our favorite toys; there are lots of toys that are roadworthy—Hitachi Magic Wands, other vibrators, wrist and ankle restraints, collars, rope, butt plugs, paddles and floggers; basically, items that won't be likely to break if they are bounced around in your luggage. There are also lots of toys that we buy when we are on the road and that should make it home in one piece. One of my favorite places for kinky toy shopping is at the Leather Market for International Mr. Leather in Chicago every Memorial Day weekend. I find some great deals from large vendors and smaller artisans. (Seriously, you *have* to go!) Just be aware that some may not make it home in one piece and buy your toys accordingly. Do you *need* a super-delicate electrical device or an antique violet wand that weekend or can you find one at home or have it shipped at a later date? Being a conscientious consumer will take the sting out of losing something. I always pack my toys in my checked luggage no matter where I go. Routinely I open up my luggage when I get to either my destination or my home and invariably I find that little card from the TSA saying how much they enjoyed going through my luggage. That way I know they have been there; it's kind of polite. So what I do to make the travel smoother is pack all my toys up on top and make them easy to get to as soon as they open the suitcase. If they are going to paw through them, I would rather they get to them easily instead of having to dig through my underwear and toiletries. Remember, they are checking for drugs and bombs. Your seven-inch stainless steel butt plug isn't a security concern, but by putting it front and center, you're making it easier for them to process your bag rather than having to dig around for it and break your camera equipment. None of my personal property has ever gone missing or been stolen or confiscated. I can't make that a broad sweeping rule, but with the amount of

Strips of three-inch-wide Velcro make great restraints—inescapable, but quickly released.

It looks like a regular case from the outside, but the TSA are going to get a surprise when they open this luggage.

traveling I do, I find the TSA to be polite and courteous, and if you behave yourself going through security checks and dress like you are on your way to visit your aunt, you will breeze through security and your stuff should arrive with you relatively unmolested. Remember: good manners never go out of style and if you get pulled into a secondary inspection and they pick up your toy, hold it out in front of them and ask you to explain, be honest and say, "That goes in my ass, sir. Um, you may want to be wearing gloves." I am going to leave it up to you, an intelligent and responsible person who bought this book so you can facilitate your sexuality, to research the rules and regulations of where you are traveling to and what you can and can't bring along, be it domestic or international. Like I said, I haven't lost anything yet and that is reason for positive optimism.

Run a cord through an ice cube tray and you get ice cube anal beads!

As we have seen, there are so many types of toys, from those you can create on the fly to some really beautiful works of art and craftsmanship you may purchase, that there is no reason to be without at least a few instruments of excitement. You are limited only by your own creative and dirty mind and remember: every toy has to have a wielder; it is the people behind them that make for a mind-blowing scene! Enjoy your toys, but never forget it is *you* who makes the scene hot and steamy. Now that we have our toys all lined up and ready, let's explore new ways of making our partner (or ourselves!) helpless so all those juicy toys can be put to good use.

Five Key Points for Playing with the Big Toys:
- Be open to new things.
- Cheap toys are twice as expensive in the long run.
- Support toy-making artisans.
- Get hands-on lessons in using electrical toys.
- Put all your kinky toys in your checked luggage when traveling by air.

Chapter Six

Advanced Bondage Techniques and Gear

If sex doesn't scare the cat, you're not doing it right.
—Anonymous

Mmm…bondage: nothing gets me hotter. You know that moment when he or she surrenders to you; how the soft closing of a pair of cuffs sounds in the bedroom when it's just the two of you? You know that little metallic click of the clasp on the D-ring that says, *You are mine now*, as you restrain her arms and legs tightly, turning her into your helpless little puddle of excitement? Submissives, you know what I am talking about as well: the way it feels to be positioned into how and what your Master desires, and then have your mobility taken away from you as you sigh a sense of relief that someone is in charge of you for as long as he desires. We love that little wriggle you do, the turn of the leg where it meets the hip that seductively beckons to be kissed with lips or a whip. Helpless, deliciously helpless. How you moan and squirm and your pussy or cock begs for attention, your chest rising and panting as

Facing Page: Hotel rooms are fun and the noises always leave your neighbors guessing.

rope bites too tightly into your flesh when you move too much. Sometimes we want you to think you can almost get away, other times we want you to stay where you are put until we are done with you. There are so many tools to bind and restrain your lover with. It doesn't have to be leather shackles; perhaps you are more of a silk scarf or rope aficionado? How about latex Vacuum Beds, leather mummy bags, plastic or veterinarian wrap? Whatever the materials used, being snugged, buckled, tied or wrapped and the physical and emotional feelings that go along with it, simply has to be experienced.

Let's take a look at some of the fun things—and some dastardly ones too—that you can do to make your slave helpless and your inner sadist amused. When I have a bondage playdate arranged, I start planning days before we get together. I ask myself what it is that I want to achieve. Do I desire to cause them helplessness, pain or discomfort? When doing bondage, ask yourself the same questions. Do you want your submissives completely immobilized or would you prefer them to be tied up so they can squirm while you do fun, bad things to them? This is not to say that you *have* to have it all planned out; in *How to Be Kinky* we saw that play partners should be flexible with their activities when scening. This helps the scene stay fluid and enjoyable rather than it being rigidly scripted, which can take the spontaneity out of playtime. Are you going to want to fuck them or have them fuck you at some point? What about squirming? Will they wriggle so much they topple off the bed trying to get away? There are a myriad of reasons to restrain someone for fun *and* safety and there are lots of fun bondage techniques to play with.

People are funny—especially when they are in bondage. It never ceases to amaze me how some people react. Some reactions can be quite opposite from their usual personalities. I have seen mouthy submissives quiet right down once they are all tied up, just like when you place a towel over a squawking parrot's cage. I have seen some normally subdued and chilled-out people get physically worked up at the challenge of bondage and fight like a calf out of a roping chute on a rodeo circuit. Forrest Gump did tell us that, "You never know what you're gonna get," but then I never saw Forrest in a hog-tie with a butt plug snug in his ass and a pair of panties jammed in his mouth. Perhaps that is in the extended DVD boxed set? If you have it, let me know.

Facing Page: Bondage in water looks both serene and amazing, but should only be attempted by the experienced.

Try running the pinwheel over your partner's hips and watch their gorgeous response.

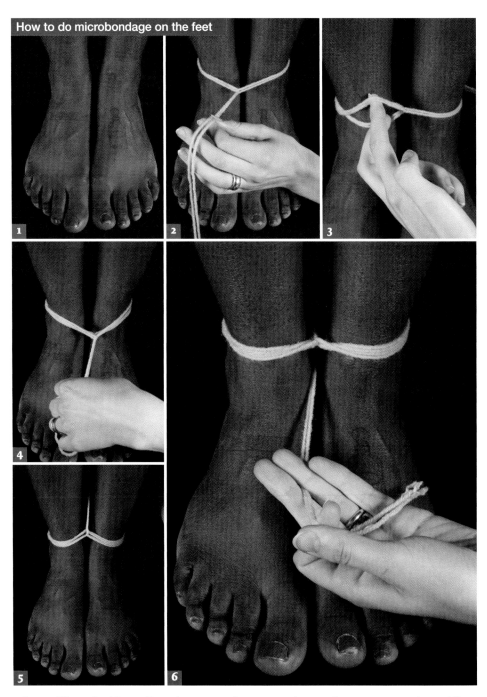

How to do microbondage on the feet

1 Get a willing pair of feet. 2 Everyday yarn works great, and comes in many pretty colors. 3 Wrap once around the legs and then pull it through the loop. 4 Make a secure knot. Any knot will do, it doesn't have to be fancy. 5 Pull the yarn up between the legs... 6 and back through underneath.

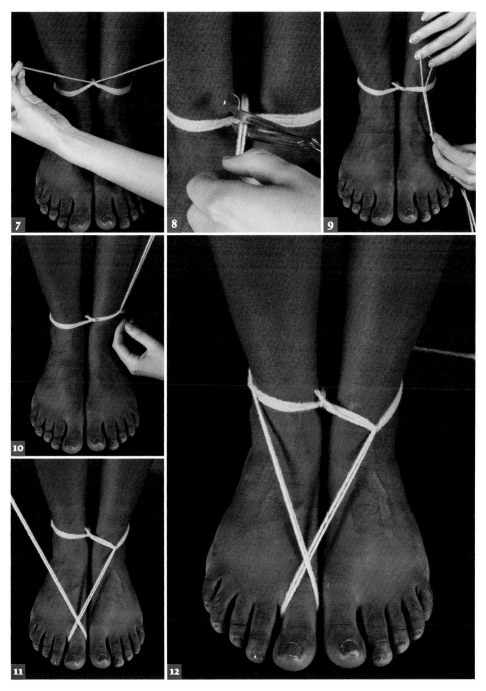

7 Make a knot tying it all together so the legs are snug. 8 Trim off the excess yarn. 9 Take a fresh piece and push a loop through the cuffs you just made and pull the ends through. 10 Snug down that loop so it becomes a knot. 11 Here is where it gets pretty. Wind the yarn around the opposite big toe... 12 then come around the back.

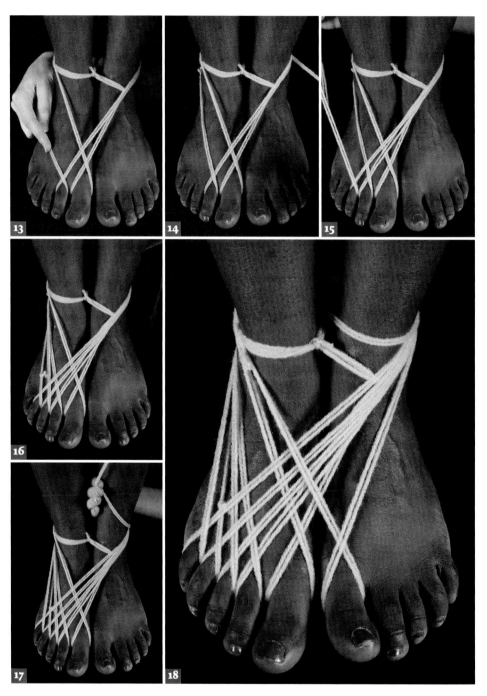

13 Capture the next toe over... 14 and again pass around the back. 15 If you start to run out of yarn, just tie some more onto it and continue. 16 Now you are getting the hang of it! 17 Continue until you trap all the toes and then pass the yarn between the legs to change direction... 18 and now come around the back and trap the big toe on the other foot.

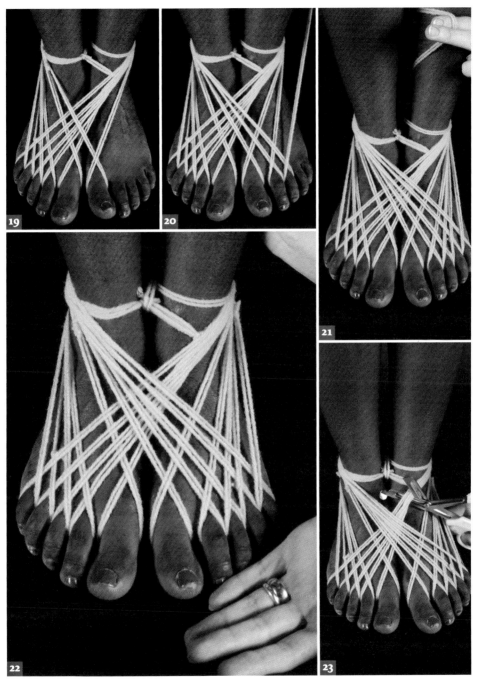

19 Make sure it is snug but not too tight, we want to be able to keep them in microbondage for as long as we like. 20 Keep repeating. 21 When you get the baby toe trapped, wind the yarn between the legs and tie it off. 22 Voila! Pretty and functional. 23 When it is time to come out, just snip it off with a pair of safety sissors, don't bother trying to untie it.

How to Be Kinkier

Invest in a wig collection. They can cheat on you with you.

Setting the Mood

Having someone helpless and delicious in front of you, or conversely being rendered helpless and delicious is one of the treasures of playtime. At that moment, possibilities, real and imagined, give you the chance to let go of your vanilla life and responsibilities. Bondage is a super way of marking the transition between your vanilla life and playtime. I love it both as a form of foreplay and as the main event. If you use it as foreplay, bondage works very well for warming up and easing someone into the playtime headspace. There is something incredibly sexy about having your partner all trussed up, ass high in the air and exposed, blindfolded and waiting with bated breath. Maybe he is starting to sweat, the small of his back glowing in anticipation. Perhaps there's a shiver that ripples through her like wind on water when you first touch her, or a soft moan escaping his lips and a sharp intake of breath that follows the scrape of your stiletto heel across his butt.

Tying someone up for sex entails some important considerations: 1) positioning and 2) safety. Lots of bondage positions are hot, sexy and challenging, but you want to be sure the position you choose suits the activities you plan to indulge in, and you want to be certain it's safe for your bottom. If you are reading this book, then I'm pretty certain you have surfed the Internet for kinky porn and stumbled across those delicious websites that have models tied up in very complex positions with every orifice plugged, crying and begging and being humiliated and all those other yummy things we love to experience in power play. I want to caution you that while those are pretty and sexy pictures, porn is a fantasy and you can't judge your own bondage and sex life by it. I have seen people struggle to recreate those types of scenes in the bedroom, where the reality may be quite different. The reality of being on a fetish porn set is one where the video camera can be turned off so more lube can be applied or the ropes can be adjusted or the hair teased again or even eyedrops squirted into the model's eyes so her mascara drips and runs down her cheeks. Not all of it is fake—some of those actors are actually into the lifestyle—but your own sex bondage can be so much hotter because it *is* real. It is you and someone you trust or love enough to be bound and fucked by and have your forehead bounced off the headboard while mounted from behind, your wrists tied tight, your nipples scraped by your lover's nails and his or her hips banging into you. I always

Facing Page: A naughty submissive sometimes needs a good spanking.

If you're new to rope bondage, try easy knots first and work your way up.

Even simple rope bondage can be beautiful.

maintain that real sex is *better* than porn and you shouldn't judge yourself by something you've seen online.

That said, online porn can serve as inspiration, but should not be your standard. There are so many positions for bondage and they all look delicious, but what the camera shows you doesn't always translate well into real-life bondage sex. A lot of what you might see online are bondage ties that concentrate on full mobility restriction rather than facilitating great sex. You should listen to your partner and keep your desires in the clouds but your feet on the ground. Rope bondage ties like the shrimp or Ebi tie are great for restriction but also allow access to your bottom's "good bits." This is a cross-legged tie that works in a few different positions—with subs on their back, their side, or if they are flexible enough, facedown and ass up for great penetrative sex. If the slave has mobility issues, a simple hands-to-knees

Be creative when thinking about your rope bondage; seek out new and interesting options.

tie will make the facedown and ass up position even more comfortable. If you love a forced blow job, then a classic Japanese bondage tie where the submissive's wrists are behind their head with their elbows tied is perfect because not only can't bottoms get away, you can use their elbows to steer.

A fresh Brazilian wax is key to getting your own way.

I love how rope bondage puts me in a place where it feels like I am being pampered by the rope top, who is spending all this time making me into his or her bondage work of art. Part of this process I love is when the bondage is both pretty and practical; for example, during sex bondage when I can't hold my legs up and open or don't want to for a really long time, but he gets me tied in that position and I can just relax into that element of control. While I am helpless and spread open, my partner can tie me in different ways and expose me or fuck me or tease me or torment me—it is all up to him and his desires. The rope allows for him to have that control over me. I can struggle and I have to confess I love to feel the rope bite into me as I struggle and squirm while they are doing whatever they want to me. The smell, the feel, the texture of rope— it all gets me hot and wet. During that struggle when the rope presses into me or pinches me sharply on the inside of my arm where the skin is tender because I struggle too much, that reminds me that I am helpless."
—Allyss, rope bottom

When you have a bottom tied up with each wrist tied to her ankles while she's on her back, you can use her for sex or even shave or wax her in preparation for your scene. Bondage for sex means you can get at their pussy, cock, ass or breasts and enjoy yourself without the rope getting in the way. If rope isn't your thing but plastic wrap is, the best part is that once you get them all wrapped up in the position you want and their naughty bits are covered, you can simply tear a hole in the plastic and enjoy. Not all bondage is for sex, but lots of kinky sex is with bondage. Once you get your partner immobilized, you never know what can transpire!

Safe and Snug

More about plastic wrap shortly, but let's revisit some basic safety first. General safety rule of thumb: the breathing and fingernail test. 1) Are they breathing, and can they tell you how they are doing? Great! Keep going. 2) If you press down on a fingernail it should turn white; when you release,

Bondage tape is easy, safe, nonthreatening to newbies, and you can make anything from cock rings to gags and masks with it!

it should turn back to pink—if that is the case, then your binds aren't too tight. Communicate. Talk to them in a sexy way. You can get all the information you need to know from nuzzling her ear while nibbling the nape of her neck and saying, "Mmm…baby, you are so hot, I love to see you squirm—are you good, everything okay?" This, rather than standing over your sub and complaining that he isn't good enough because the tie you did with his arms jacked up behind him has caused those limbs to fall asleep and he's complaining about it. Keep the mood, and you will keep the scene while you readjust your knots or rope.

Once I did a scene where I tied two sexy ladies together on a bed at a local fetish night. One was an experienced bottom of mine, and the other was new. I had gone through the pre-scene negotiation with her about any issues that might arise or could affect our time together. She assured me over and over that she was good to go. I did an elaborate body harness on her and had her hands tied behind her back. Suddenly she went into a panic attack—her breath rate increased, she started sweating and struggling. I calmed her down and untied her hands. Because I build my bondage in modular layers, I was able to untie her hands immediately and didn't have to untie her body harness. Once as her hands were free she calmed down immediately; we gave her some water and sat reassuring her. That was all it took to help relieve her stress. We didn't even have to untie the complex body harness. She was so excited to finally be tied up by me that she didn't tell me about her anxiety for fear that I wouldn't play with her. That put me in a potentially difficult position. If I had known of her issues ahead of time, I would have done the tie differently. After a break we were able to get back into a lighter scene and we all enjoyed ourselves. Lesson to submissives: let your Top know any health-related issues you have: asthma, epilepsy, a painful joint, anxiety, et cetera. It doesn't mean we won't play with you, it just means we may have to adjust our scene accordingly. Let us do the driving, but give us a "car" in which we know all the controls. Any quality Dominant, Mistress, Master or Top will want your safety to be of paramount importance. If this is not the case, then you should reevaluate the person who wants to do something to you. Breaking our toys means never getting to play with them again. Speak up; don't be shy if you have a trick knee from a high school field hockey injury that suddenly jumps out of joint, or if you get light-headed when excited. Everybody wants open communication when it comes to health-related issues. Play should be fun but safety is serious.

Playing rope bondage games with a super flexible partner will take you places you never dreamed.

How to put someone in a leather mummy bag

1 Get a sexy submissive and open the bag all the way to the feet. This particular one from Northbound Leather features a two way zipper and reinforced seams. **2** On the inside of the bag you will find arm sleeves that zip up to the armpit. This is so they can't fuss with the zipper from the inside. **3** Then zip up the bag from the bottom to the top. **4** Leather breathes more than plastic so you can have longer sessions in it.

Full-Body Bondage

Plastic wrap you get from the grocery store or better yet from a packing and moving supply store is so much fun for under twenty dollars! I have had many playdates that wound up with my partner all wrapped up like a burrito. There are a few safety issues you need to know about when wrapping someone in plastic. The first one is their temperature. If you use a rectal thermometer to check, suddenly you have a medical play scene! You don't really need a thermometer, though; you can check by touching them, or simply asking them how they are feeling. When you wrap someone up, it causes his or her body to be more sensitive to temperature change. By wrapping them with plastic, you are using an impervious membrane that doesn't allow moisture to escape, so depending on the ambient temperature, this can cause them to sweat—especially if you have an evil gleam in your eye and threaten them with a chili pepper enema.

Second, when you wrap someone, each subsequent layer of wrapping becomes tighter, compressing his or her body. Placing a tea towel between the bony parts of the body will make it much more comfortable for them to stay in the bondage longer. Between the knees is one of the key locations. Always make someone comfortable until *you* decide it is time for him or her to be uncomfortable. Not having to compete with distracting pain will keep their attention focused on you and what is happening to them. A fine alternative for snuggly wrapping and containing someone has been dreamed up by companies like Northbound Leather that produce hand-stitched and riveted, full-leather mummy bags. These bags have these advantages: 1) they are ready to go *now* when you are feeling horny instead of having to fuss with plastic wrap; 2) they have internal sleeves for the arms; 3) you can get your partner into and out of them in hurry, and 4) they are made from leather, which breathes with the body so the chances of overheating are lessened.

There is also duct tape mummification—again, the membrane is impervious, so treat it like plastic wrap, but first wrap the victim in a layer of plastic so when it comes time to remove the duct tape you don't have to peel them like a banana. That would be terrible aftercare. The people who love duct tape really love it. There are bottoms who become sexually aroused just from the smell of duct tape.

Something that has enjoyed a resurgence over the past few years due to new designs as new technology has become available is the Vacuum

Girls, being on the receiving end for years doesn't mean you are a natural at fucking with a strap-on. Positioning is everything.

Your partner isn't a mind reader: you have to let him or her know what turns you on.

Bed. Imagine being sheathed entirely in latex, hugged tight and frozen in place with a second skin sucked tightly to your skin, with position changes easily made by simply loosening the gasket around the neck. I really love making someone completely helpless in a Vacuum Bed and at the mercy of my Hitachi Magic Wand. I vividly remember the first time I saw an image of a latex Vacuum Bed in action: a woman was encased in shiny black latex, all of her curves, every nook completely defined and visible, the pattern on her fishnet stockings sharp, yet she was completely restrained and encapsulated by this sexy and shiny thin latex second skin. She was beautiful, sexy and intriguing. In essence a Vacuum Bed is a large, rectangular, airtight, latex bag. This is hooked to a regular vacuum cleaner that sucks all of the air out, trapping anyone who is in there between the two layers of latex sheeting. The latex sucks down to perfectly fit the user; no fussing with sizes, no hunting for the right frame—they fit everyone. Think Han Solo in Carbonite, but way sexier. Some beds have a breathing tube or a hole, and for the claustrophobic, a tapered neck gasket like a turtleneck sweater is available. Inside the bag a frame of plastic pipes sucks out the air while keeping the bag stretched out tight and flat. That is what it is, but what it does is something else entirely.

Being inside a Vacuum Bed really isn't as scary as it looks. The best thing about Vacuum Beds is that unlike rope, binders, cuffs and manacles, the Vacuum Bed binds you all over. There are no points of high stress; no straps that dig in, no chafing. When inside, the only thing that you'll have control over is the pose you strike. My advice to someone trying out a bed for the first time—pick an easy pose. You'll have a lot more fun if you're in a comfortable position but bear in mind you want your partner to have access to your fun bits! Throw a pillow under your head or a foam sheet under or inside the bed for extra comfort. The next part is the really exciting sensation when the vacuum is turned on and all the latex sucks down on you. First it starts to slowly conform to your body and then very rapidly sucks you down so you're immobilized. That's usually the part where you start giggling with delight. Think of it as a full-body latex hug.

So you're stuck in the bed... You can wiggle a little, but you are basically confined to your starting position. You'll be able to feel almost everything through the latex. It's very sensitive to hot and cold and only slightly dulls physical sensations so it's still great for impact play and vibrators!
—Archean, of Kink Engineering

Showertime has never been more fun.

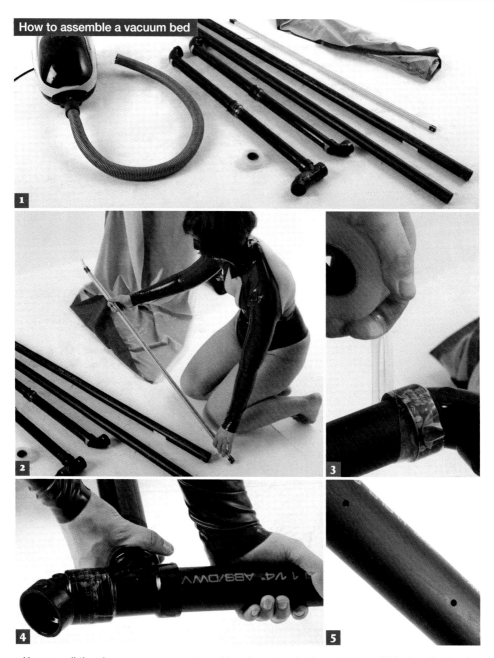

How to assemble a vacuum bed

1 Here are all the pieces: one vacuum, two side rails and end rails made from PVC pipe, the bar for sealing it, the latex bed itself and some tape. 2 Unroll the latex bag and start assembling the bed. 3 Use a low tac semi stretchy tape to tape the frame bits together. This will help keep the frame solid. We like clear hockey tape available at any sports store. 4 On the bottom rail there will be one joint that points outwards. This is where the vacuum attaches to. 5 When you assemble the side rails, make sure the holes are pointing inwards.

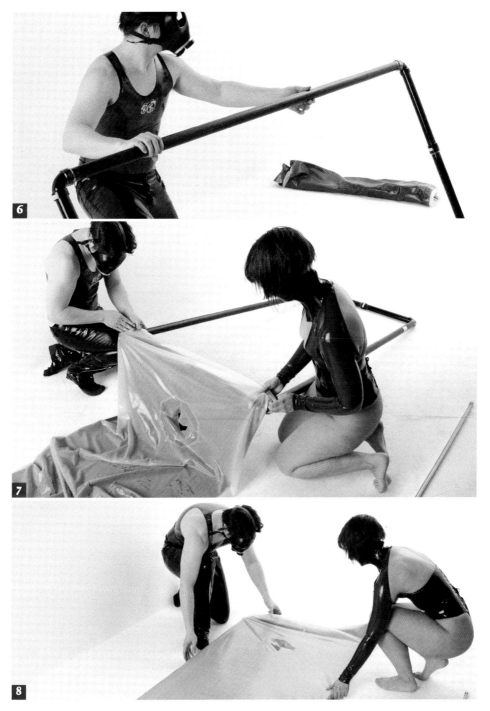

6 Once all the joints are taped, lay it out. 7 Insert the frame into the latex bed, being careful not to rip the latex. 8 All the way to the end. If it is a bed with a zipper it will fit the frame perfectly. If it is a bed with a closure bar it will have 8 extra inches at the top.

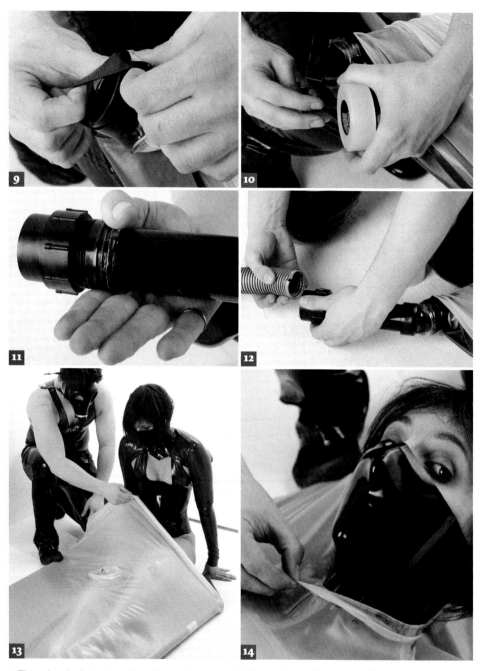

9 There is a hole designed to fit over the one joint that points outwards. 10 Make sure you tape this too. 11 Kink Engineering has created a simple one way valve that means you only have to run the vacuum intermittently. 12 Tape that joint and fit it into the vacuum hose. 13 Get your submissive to slide into the bed. 14 Make sure the neck gasket is smoothed out.

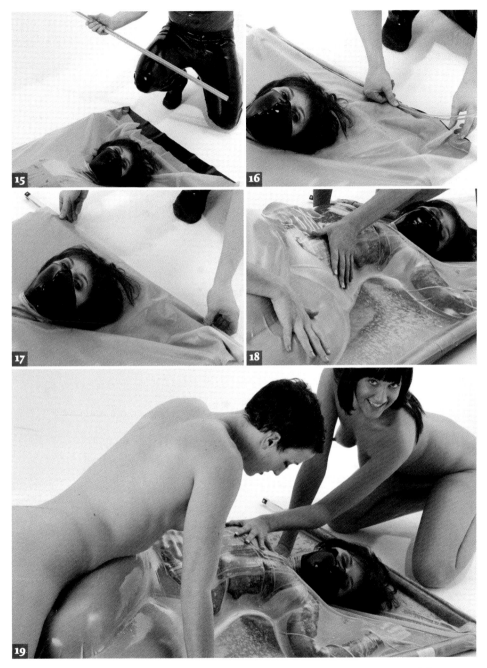

15 The closure bar is a fast and easy way to get someone in and out of the bed, much better than the zippers of old style beds. 16 Lay the bar under the latex, and then firmly push the tube into the slot, sealing the bag. 17 Roll it up for neatness and to ensure the best seal possible. 18 Turn on the vacuum and let it suck all the air out. Then get some lovely slaves to lube up your victim... 19 and body slide alllll over them!

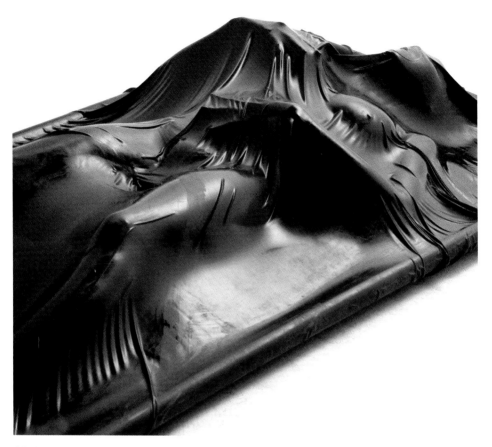

Climbing out of a vac bed can be just as much fun as climbing in.

Forced sex is fabulous, but he/she has to be willing.

The Vacuum Beds produced today are of a superior quality to the ones made five, ten or fifteen years ago. Silk-screening and multiple colors have pimped up this fun toy and made it so much less intimidating than the ones your parents played in. (Weird picture, I know, but an intriguing thought that might explain a lot about you.) Assembling a Vacuum Bed is easy with quick connectors.

One of my favorite companies, Kink Engineering, has created new and superior gasket seals that are more secure, and a valve that doesn't require the vacuum to be run constantly.

Fun Tips for Enjoying a Vacuum Bed

■ Changing positions: ass up, arms behind back, fingers in hair; fingers close to erogenous zones—but not touching

■ Run ice cubes over the bed and watch your partner squirm!

■ Before lubricating the outside of the bed, run your fingers along the surface, applying a bit of pressure. This will cause the latex to pinch at your partner's skin a bit

■ Put a vibrator inside the Vacuum Bed—your partner will beg you to turn it on, and then later beg you to turn it off!

■ Lubricate the inside of the bed and allow your partner to slowly slide around inside and then turn the vacuum on and off at different intervals to surprise him

■ Put a sheet or thin layer of foam rubber under your partner inside the Vacuum Bed and notice that she can't move *at all* as the bed gets even more rigid with the added nonstretchy material in there

■ At a party, invite your friends to give massages. Vacuum Bed massages are about as close to heaven as you can get on earth

■ Tickling your sub while he or she is inside is about as close to hell as you can get on earth—fun, fun hell

■ Add blindfold and earplugs or a gasmask to an open-faced Vacuum Bed and you can have a very complete sensory deprivation experience. A great way to hypersensitize your sub to your every touch.

■ Lube up the outside and have naked sexy people slide all over your sub. (My personal favorite!)

When pegging your partner with a strap-on, start with him bent over the edge of the bed and then work your way into a more standard face-to-face position until you are comfortable with the dildo and know how it will move with you.

All of this adds up to an extra dimension in your kinky bondage play. You have a perfect latex form of your partner as a living sculpture to satisfy or deny; watch the desperate bottom try to squirm away or toward your attentions with little success. Tease them, tickle them, suck, ride and caress them and send them over the edge into ecstasy; it's all in your hands.

The Right to Remain Silent: Metal Restraints

I know many people who love handcuffs and metal restraints. They are hard, sometimes shiny, sexy and have that classic, "Oh, I have been a bad boy, Officer Roslyn, what are you going to do about it?" feel to them.

For a lot of us, handcuffs picked up in a novelty store were the first things that we used to restrain or be restrained in bed with. For a lot of us they are our entry point into realizing how much fun restraint is. Their biggest benefit is their immediacy. That is the reason law enforcement uses

Handcuffs—a bondage classic.

them—they can be quickly put on, and when you're doing a hot takedown scene where the two of you are wrestling around on the ground, they give of an air of authority that is pretty fucking hot once snapped on. What I am not a big fan of is how unyielding they are. The more someone struggles, the more they can do some serious damage to all the nerves and tendons in his or her wrists. Now, I can hear those metal restraint lovers out there about to jump on their soapboxes about how you have to apply them properly or get the right style and so on, but let me reassure you that while it can be seen as a drawback to the safety issue, this is also one of their strengths. One of the styles of play I really love is "compliance training"—when I put someone in a position, I want her to remain in that position for as long as I desire. Failure to do so will result in very painful consequences.

Handcuffs and other metal restraints are wonderful for compliance training because of their very unyielding nature. If someone does struggle, the edges of the cuffs will bite very painfully into the soft, tender part of his wrists. That much said, handcuffs don't lend themselves very well to the

Some dildos make better plugs than strap-ons. Think about the shape and material for what you want to penetrate and where!

Facing Page: A sub and dom should complement each other in all ways.

Wrist shackles have a touch of the 19th Century about them and are super sexy for this reason.

myriad of other positions that we typically play with in the lifestyle. Hand-cuffed hands above the head, twisting while being spanked or whipped, or even worn during sex will push on the blood vessels and nerves. If you are looking for cuffs, buy high-quality ones that can be double cuffed—meaning they have a locking device built in so that they can't be tightened by an overzealous "arresting officer" or tighten on their own while roughhousing with them on. And for the love of god, keep a spare key on your key chain with your car keys, just in case. It is easy to lose a little handcuff key while playing, but most of us can remember where we put our car keys.

The other style of metal cuffs are shackles and irons. Flat and wide, they distribute the force that is exerted across a wider surface area.

If someone struggles wearing these, they don't have as much "bite" as handcuffs, but they have another benefit—the weight of the chains. These are more for endurance sessions. Do you have a sassy and spitfire submissive on your hands for a playdate? Bring out the irons and chains and make him haul them around for an hour; it will take the piss and vinegar out of him, which is very convenient for you. Typically irons and chains will either come with a hex key threaded nut to lock them or a standard lock. Choose the style that is best for you, but if you need to get your slave out of them in a hurry, you better know where you put the key.

Also, just to reiterate the biggest all-time safety rule in bondage—never leave someone who is bound, shackled or cuffed alone. We want the chance to play again and again with someone special and building trust gives you both an opportunity for it to grow it deeper and to explore your bondage desires further with each other. As I said earlier in the chapter, play should fun, but safety should be serious. The next chapter will take a more in depth look at practices that will keep everyone safe.

Kinky sex should be fun! Take your needs seriously, but remember that it is okay to laugh about mishaps. Look back and talk about things together so you can make things better for next time.

Five Key Points for Taking Your Bondage Further:

■ Set the mood.

■ Your bondage sex life can be better than what you see online because it is with someone you care about.

■ If you are going to tie them up to fuck 'em, don't put the rope in the way.

■ Metal restraints look delicious but can be painful.

■ Latex Vacuum Beds are awesome!

Chapter Seven

Better safe...

Safety is something that happens between your ears, not something you hold in your hands.
—Jeff Cooper

In *How to Be Kinky*, we looked at basic safety issues: how to be and stay safe as you introduce kinky fun into your life. The upshot was and still is this: play should be fun, but safety should be serious. This time we'll go a bit more in depth. Presumably, you picked up this book because you want to know more of the deliciously dirty things that can happen in the bedroom dungeon. You might be beyond the newbie stage and more than ready to introduce heavier activities into your playtime, but with heavier play the risk increases, and so the responsibilities become heavier too. I personally love edge play. I love to walk that razor-thin line, balancing along it as I step lightly while dangling someone beneath me over the abyss. To know my play partner is excited, turned on and a little scared gives my play a charged edge that really brings all of the things I love about kinkier play together into one beautifully wrapped-up package. But I would not walk that line if I felt that I could not be responsible about safety. I wouldn't go rock climbing without a rope; you wouldn't go scuba diving without a buddy and you certainly wouldn't go to a mall on Christmas Eve without a girlfriend to watch your back, even if all the shoes were 75 percent off. Managing the risks of kinkier play successfully will set you apart from the wannabe players and place you among those who are respected in the scene.

Risk Management

Nothing is perfectly safe. There is inherent risk in all that we do, and this is especially true in BDSM. Risk management is about identifying, assessing and prioritizing risks in the face of uncertainty followed by steps to reduce

Facing Page: Yarn is great for microbondage in the pool.

183

Playing safe is key so you can really let yourself go and be at the mercy of someone else.

When lingerie shopping, take your partner into the changing room with you.

or minimize unforeseen circumstances in playtime. There are no failsafe systems, so we have to minimize the risk as best we can. Your partner needs to know the risks that are involved with heavier play whether he or she is receiving or administering it. There has been a lot written over the years about Safe Sane and Consensual and R.A.C.K. (Risk Aware Consensual Kink), two schools of thought concentrating on safety. While there is ongoing debate about one versus the other, what is important is not that there is one system better than the other, but that we educate ourselves and become aware that the activities we are engaging in come with an inherent risk, some heavier than others. Think of getting kinkier as an extreme sport—more thrilling, more adventurous, but also more risky.

One thing I don't do is play with anyone who has the mindset of "I am so tough I have never called my safeword!" and takes a lot of pride in that. There is an undercurrent of selfishness in this attitude. As the dominant, you could unknowingly push too far and do damage without this person calling his safeword, and who do you think is going to be on the receiving end of assault charges after that same individual has had a day or two to realize just how bruised or damaged he is? Some people use kink as a way

Kinkier play is more risky—which is half the fun!

to be hurt to cover up for some unresolved issue in their past, though they may or may not be actively aware of it. We have all seen drama queens (both boys and girls) and we know how much they love to stir up the pot just to get attention. As an experienced player I need to know that the bottom is capable and well adjusted enough to use her safeword if the situation warrants it. Though it may not seem like it at time, both partners are vulnerable in any heavier scene; a Top's safety shouldn't be put in jeopardy because of someone's ego. Questions I always ask myself before I play with new partners include:

- Do they have a positive outlook on life and are they fun to be around?
- Do they treat their body with respect or do they abuse drugs and alcohol?
- Is their life filled with drama or are they compassionate toward others?
- Are they patient or do they want everything right now?

Conversely, the submissive needs to check in with any potential dominants about their style of play and if they are going to ask them to go farther than they are comfortable with. Every scene should give you a chance to push your boundaries, a chance to grow and learn new and interesting aspects of

Wearing stockings and heels without panties will always get your partner's attention.

185

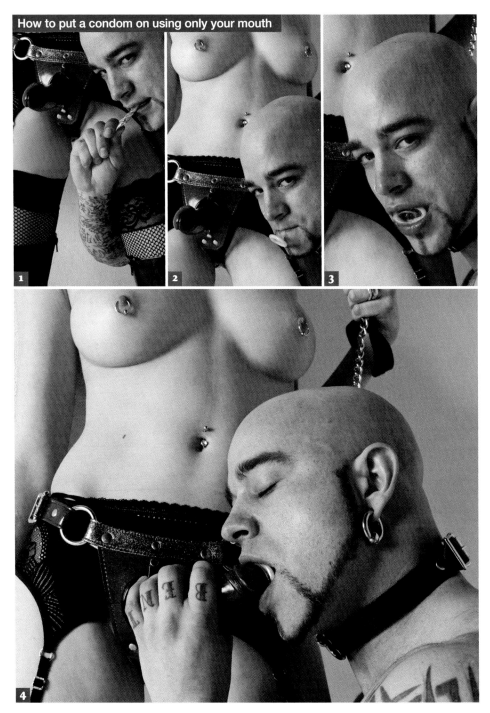

How to put a condom on using only your mouth

1 Open the wrapper and pull it out into your mouth. 2 Make sure the end is the right way out and is in the tip of your mouth. 3 Gently pull it into your mouth and hold the ring with your lips.
4 Get a good hold of that shaft and push the end onto the head.

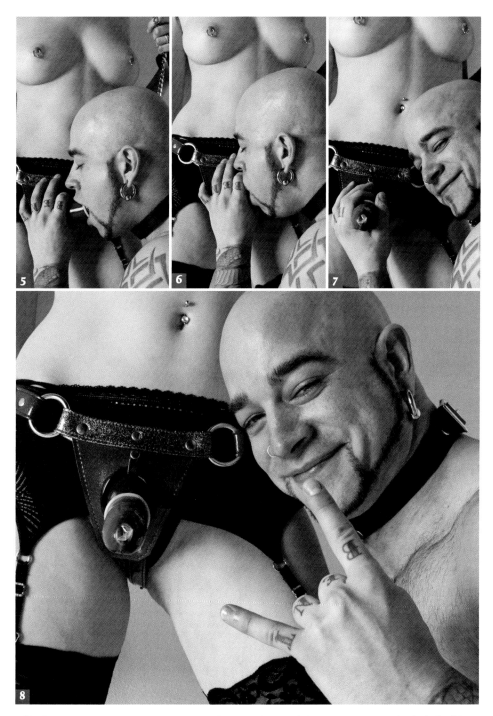

5 Begin to roll the condom one with your lips, pushing firmly but gently so you don't rip it. 6 As you push down the shaft, keep rolling it on with your lips... 7 all the way to the base, then use your fingers to make it nice and neat. 8 Ready to rock!

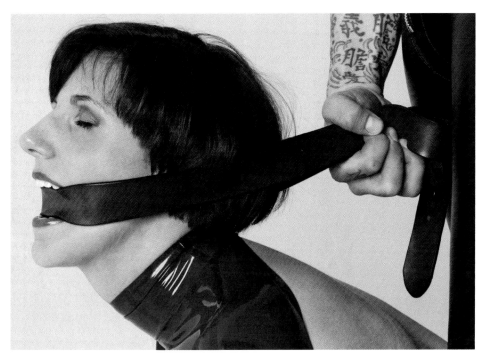

Some toys have negative connotations for partners. Make sure you know what your playmate is comfortable with and what they aren't.

yourself, but you should never be forced into your "no-go zone" by yourself or anyone else. Safewords are there for a reason—never let your ego get in the way of using them. If you use yours no one will think less of you—either as the Top or the bottom. Others will respect you for knowing your boundaries and wanting to explore *within* them. Growing up in a family that raised horses, I remember how my dad used to say, "There are acres in the field for the horses to run; only the dumb ones keep running into the fence." Running into the fence inadvertently is to be expected occasionally, but to keep throwing yourself against it in hopes of a different outcome is pretty lame. A perfect example of this in the scene is an occasion on which I watched a friend of mine continue to beat his submissive with his belt in the playroom, event after event, even though "the belt" had a negative association with her past growing up. She would always accept it begrudgingly but then for the rest of the event she would be distant, removed and not particularly social or talkative. And he could never figure out why she wasn't as chatty and social

Facing Page: When you find the perfect partner the possibilities are endless!

People's pain tolerances can be very different—and it can be very sexy to push those limits, but go slowly.

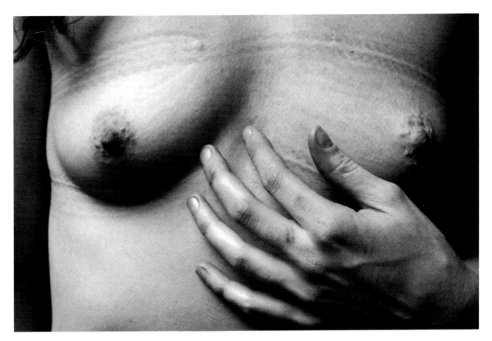

Rope bondage will leave some beautiful marks on the body.

after the scene as when they first arrived, regardless of her trying to communicate with him that the belt wasn't for her.

Choosing your play partner is an active pursuit, not something that should be reactive, and you shouldn't just play with whoever wanders into your life. How someone acts in his or her regular life is a pretty clear indication of his behavior when playtime comes around. Quality over quantity of experiences will really help you in building your kinky life, and keep you safe as you explore and advance. Being aware that kinkier sex comes with bigger risks should keep you researching, taking classes and workshops and learning how to manage that risk.

Managing Your Risk:
Questions to Ask Yourself Ahead of Playtime

■ Is this activity for me or for someone else?
■ Is it within my physical/mental and emotional comfort zone?
■ If it is just outside that comfort zone, how comfortable am I in exploring it with my partner?
■ Can I do this and still be safe?

Blindfold and then strip your partner when you get home, pose her on all fours in the living room and tell her to stay still and wait until you are ready.

- Will my safewords be respected?
- Is there aftercare involved if I need it?
- Is that piece of equipment safe/sturdy/able to support me properly?

Be dynamic and responsive to change as you evolve and grow. You are responsible for your safety in choosing a partner and your activities. Choose your path with an active sense of responsibility since you are the one to ultimately live with your choices.

If a Scene Goes Sideways

- Stay calm and stop the activity you are doing.
- Talk to your partner in a reassuring tone.
- Fix the problem.

Sometimes we can step on a trigger in our partners without knowing it. Work on your communication so they feel they have a voice in what is happening and when.

Kinky sex can be therapeutic, but it is not therapy.

Pain in the Ass

Pain is normal for the body; it is a response that tells our brain something is wrong. It is a perfect defense system to tell us, "Hey, knock it off!" when there is something trying to harm us. However, one of the fun things we do in kinky sex is to explore just where our fine line is in regard to how much pain we can take. We push our boundaries, nudge them farther, and sweat through the tough parts to get to that flush of endorphins. Figuring out where that line is can be a revealing experience, but I want to help you figure out how to make that personal growth happen safely. Pain is subjective and no pain should be taken lightly. Some people have a very high tolerance for pain but for others, the threshold is much lower. Interestingly, research has indicated that women seem to be much more tolerant of pain and seem to achieve an endorphin high easier than men, possibly because of the connection to being able to withstand childbirth. However, that doesn't mean you can go to town on your female play partner with no warm-up or go as hard as you can. You have to be an excellent judge of

Facing Page: This sexy ass might need a bit of a rest after this session!

Spanking on the fleshy parts of the body such as the ass won't leave serious bruises.

what your partner can take and when. How much is too much for you, and how much is just enough is something you will understand with experience and time. Environment and context also have to do with how well a person is prepared to receive pain. When you are hot and sweaty and super turned on and every nerve in your body is alight, you can take much more intense sensations than when you are not turned on. It is important for your partner to understand that you need to be warmed up and not just jump from zero to sixty in the span of a few minutes. The top wants to get as much out of the scene as the masochist does, and timing, environment and warming up the body all play a huge role in creating a fun scene and achieving that fabled experience called "subspace"—that moment where the bottom gets a flush of endorphins through his or her body.

When it comes to kinky sex, have you ever been so excited that you were drip-ping with anticipation or had a scene so hot you felt you were floating? That is very likely due to endorphins flooding your system. Conversely, did you ever have really bad aftercare that didn't feel right? That could be from the lack of endorphins. Your body relies on its sugar supply to create endorphins and we need that sugar supply replaced after playing, otherwise it can lead to feelings of letdown, lethargy, headaches, shakes or a temperature drop.

Before a scene I will ask a submissive or slave what they have eaten and when, and if they have not taken in enough sugar and nutrients, I will have them do so, and give it time to settle before we play, I will also refuel that sugar supply in a timely but not too quick manner after playing. This is no guarantee that you will reach subspace but it increases your chances of producing endor-phins that can take you there.

—Boss Bondage, BDSM educator, body piercer and sadist

Let your partner push you onto the ground and stand over you while you masturbate for him/her.

The Bruise Brothers

We consensually hit each other in kinky sex, and chances are one of you is going to end up with a few lovely bruises. It is one of those fun things we do that serve as reminders for a few days after of what a great time we had!

But what causes a bruise and what can you do to make it fade faster if you have a job interview a few days after a play session, and you don't want anyone to see those marks on your leg or arms? What causes bruising is contusion: the area struck has turned a different color and is a little raised and sore. Bruising is the second most common injury in sports after strains. While not considered serious, bruises are going to be sore and dis-color the skin for a week or so. When something strikes your skin, the soft tissue under your skin is crushed but the skin isn't broken; when this tissue is crushed, blood leaks out from ruptured capillaries and pools under the skin. This is what causes that red or brown or purple mark and makes it "ouchy" to press on. There are three different categories of bruises:

■ First degree: minor rupture, a little color, soreness and maybe a bit of stiffness.

■ Second degree: moderate rupture—increased bleeding under the skin, more purple discoloration and increased swelling. There is also pain and a moderate loss of movement at the site.

■ Third degree: severe rupture—major bleeding of the capillaries and mas-sive swelling; extreme pain or instability around the site.

Kinky sex can burn 380 calories in an hour. Conversely, cum only has about 5 calories if you swallow.

The first two degrees a person can have a much easier recovery from. Within a week or so, the body should be pretty much back to normal. With the third degree we are dealing with some severe injuries and I don't recommend that anybody indulge in play that will cause severe injury. As I often say, we don't want to break the people we play with; that way we can play again and again and again. Let's wear our bruises like trophies from a stellar weekend of kinky sex, but not end up in the hospital. It is also important to recognize that everyone bruises differently. This is dependent on age, health and elasticity of the skin. Some people may not bruise much as a result of an over-the-knee spanking, while others will from the exact same sensations. As we age our blood vessels become more fragile, and typically age is a large factor in the speed of healing time, though not always. Degree and duration of bruising largely have to do with a person's overall health. It is imperative to know how someone's body is going to react to your "administrations," when you play, so that you don't make them look like they fell off a cliff in the Amazonian rainforest, hit a waterfall on the way down, ricocheted off an alligator or two and washed up on the shore at your feet. For instance, I have found that caning can produce as wide a spectrum of bruising as the variety of people receiving it. From the exact same force I exert with a cane across say, three or four bottoms, I will get just as many different lasting marks. Some will bruise minimally, while others will have an ass as purple as Barney the dinosaur (now there is someone who needs a fucking ball gag and a caning).

But what happens if you need to minimize bruising after a play session and how do you speed up the healing time? If you know that a speedier healing timeline is needed after a hard play session, you only have to look to a typical first aid course for what to do: *R.I.C.E.* **R**est the bum or body and keep it still, put some **I**ce on it to reduce the swelling, wrap it to give it some **C**ompression and **E**levate the limb. (Mm, ass up and face down!) You can build all of this into an extended aftercare scene. Once you take your slave down from the stocks where he has endured a delicious whipping for you, bundle him up and lay him in a nice quiet spot. Get him to sit his bum on some ice packs (this is its own form of torture) or some frozen peas. Peas aren't normally sexy, but I'm sure you can figure out a way to include them in your scene. When putting the ice on the

Facing Page: Everyone loves to be at the mercy of a sexy Top with a flogger.

Men are visual creatures. They need to be shown. Take your dildo or favorite sex toy and show them what you like and how you like it.

sore spot, make sure you put a barrier between the bottom's flesh and the ice—a damp cloth or the plastic bag that the peas come in. The last thing you want to do is give him frostbite and damage the skin even more. Let the bottom use his or her best judgment as to how long the ice should stay on the area. Ten to twenty minutes is a good guideline, putting it on and taking it off. If the affected area is a limb or thigh, you can compress it with Veterinarian wrap, a cheap elastic bandage type of wrap that sticks to itself, available in all kinds of pretty colors. Every toy bag should have some. The compression will reduce the swelling and bleeding under the skin.

It is important to exercise the area the next day. If you are the submissive and your thighs and ass are all bruised, you really do need to be up and moving around the day after: movement will cause the blood to circulate through the bruised area and help speed up the healing process. In addition to basic first aid, there are also topical creams available that will help speed up the healing. My favorite two that are readily available are Arnica cream or an over-the-counter ointment called Traumeel, applied approximately two to three times a day. Most importantly, wait until the area is fully healed before playing hard on that area again.

Rope bondage aficionados will experience a different form of bruising, one that results from compression of the rope on the body and will happen sometimes after a hard and rough rope scene. You may notice red dots under the skin, right around the area that was tied hard. These are called Petechiae, and if caused from rope play, this isn't any greater a concern than regular bruising. The blood has leaked from the capillaries into the skin and the spots are quite tiny—about one to three millimeters—and don't change color when you press on them. Treat them as you would any regular bruise: use some Arnica cream on them and they will disappear in a few days. If they appear not as a result of hard play, then you need to seek professional medical advice since they could be indicators of a more serious condition.

People who have tattoos and who like to be played with hard may be concerned that bruising will affect their tattoo. I have done research into this subject and at this point I can say that a first- or second-degree bruise won't affect a tattoo since the ink is inside your skin. I can't speak for a third-degree bruise, but I would imagine that if your body is in that much trauma, a tattoo should be the least of your concerns.

With rope bondage, your only limit is your own imagination.

Rope Bondage: Safe and Spectacular

There is something so very sexy and transcendent about tying up your lovers, or wrestling with them and then hog-tying them. I have had the opportunity to tie and lash many wonderful people over the years, experiences that have added to my personal growth as a Dominant and as an artist. My friends the Knotty Boys have written several useful books on rope bondage, both how to do it and how to make the knots pretty, and I highly encourage you to pick up their books and see what is in them for yourself. For the purposes of this chapter I am going to go over some safety tips and tricks you should be aware of that will help round out your own evolution as a rope bondage aficionado.

Picture this: the stage is set in a downtown club; a suspension cube and rigging points are set up and I lead my performance partner out onstage with the rope leash pulling her along on all fours. The stage is dark, but my

A rope body harness, or karada, is beautiful both in and out of bed.

fingers are deft and quickly pull my ropes through the suspension ring, and soon I have her dangling and swinging before the crowd. I spin and twirl her, swaying her back and forth under the purple and neon lights in rhythm to the music, and when finished, I lower her to the ground in a delicious heap before pulling her offstage. This is what the audience sees. What they don't see is all the prep work I have done ahead of time. I have pre-tied her hip harness that is the same color as her outfit so that it blends into the background. I have coiled my ropes so they will unspool with a simple shake, and I have them placed on a small table near the suspension rig so I can grab them as I need them, all arranged in a specific order from shortest to longest. I am methodical in my approach to safety: my safety shears are tucked in my back pocket and my carabineers have their gates opened and are clipped to the front of my pants pockets. My bootlaces are tied tight; I have tucked in my pant cuffs because I know once I start tying and the rope is flying there are a multitude of unknown variables that can creep up and

Facing Page: Multiple line rope suspension creates a more comfortable experience.

try to snag my rope and spoil the performance—perhaps an exposed bolt on the rig by the DJ table or a snag in the wooden floor of the stage. Then as my rope is put on and layered, there is a definite tripping hazard as it winds and attempts to get caught under my feet or my partner's high heels.

Whether it is a stage performance or a private experience in the bedroom, playing with rope is sexy and fun, but there are definitely some safety points you should be aware of. Tripping hazards are definitely one of them. Ever have a cat in the same room as you tried to tie up your partner? Try it and see what happens; that is an interesting extra variable that you don't anticipate initially. Don't rush, make the scene fun and playful and take your time. We don't want to get so tangled up that we trip and fall. One thing I see happen with people new to rope bondage is "whip eye"—where you are so excited and moving so quickly that you pull the rope through a chest harness too fast and the end whips out when you pull it and flicks the bottom in the face. That is annoying at best and can damage his or her eye at worst. Slow it down or seductively put your hand up as a shield as you pull the rope free.

Have your partner move when you tell him to move: standing, sitting or lying down? A nice soft bed is much easier to play on and more forgiving than a hard wooden stage in an underground club. The body has many pressure points and tying knots over top of them will cause a lot of discomfort. Let's keep the knots over the meaty parts of the body—like the tummy or chest or on the forearms and legs. I won't tie a rope over the top of a joint on someone's body because there are too many exposed nerves and there isn't much meat over those areas. You should always have a pair of safety shears nearby in case your partner needs to be cut out. If you are going to use hemp rope for bondage where the submissive will be wet, for instance if you plan on hosing him down in the shower, be aware that the hemp will swell the knots shut and constrict his body as it tightens the wetter it gets. If you don't have a pair of pliers or a very strong marlin spike to untie your play partner, you will be cutting your rope to get him out. I always recommend that if the rope is going to get wet, be sure to use a nylon-based rope, which will not swell when soaked.

One last issue I want to mention is something I teach rope players how to avoid in my hog-tie class—positional asphyxia. This has sometimes been the cause of death in suspects arrested by the police and put into a hog-tie position with their legs up and their hands cuffed behind their

How to coil a rope

1 First step – pick up one end and run the rope through your hands as you gather it in loose coils... 2 then drop the bundle on the ground and find the two ends and bring them together. 3 Hold the two ends together by pinching your thumb over them in the palm of your hand. 4 You are going to form what is known as a 'butterfly coil." You lay the rope back and forth across your hand in nice easy to manage loops that are evenly spaced. 5 Note that you aren't winding the rope around anything, just laying it back and forth across your palm.

6 Keep going until you have about almost all the rope laid in your hand and have about a 3' tail left. 7 Now carefully grip your rope bundle and turn your hand over. The rope should fold on itself and hang from its middle now. 8 Now grab that bundle by its middle and let go with your other hand. 9 Take the 3' tail and start winding it around the bundle nice and tight. 10 Let the winding start at the bottom and move towards the top.

11 Lay them nice and flat, don't cross over the wraps. 12 Here is the tricky part. When you have about 1 foot left, make one last wrap around and go over your outstretched finger... 13 then fold that last foot of rope in half... 14 and stick the middle part of it through that loop you just made with your outstretched finger. 15 Once it is through halfway, start to tighten the whole set of wraps without pulling it all the way through. This is so you can just pull on the end of the loop and the whole bundle will come undone without any tangles. 16 Voila! Just like this, a nice tight bundle that is easily stored in your toy bag and will be ready when you need it.

Outdoor bondage in a private area is exciting and liberating.

back while lying on a hard surface. Hog-ties are fun: I love them, you love them, and we want to keep playing with them, so pay attention to the surface that the rope bottom will be lying on. On a hard surface the person's diaphragm will have a hard time working after about fifteen minutes. I recommend that people play with hog-ties on a nice soft bed or couch or a whole bunch of pillows. If the bottom's breathing becomes labored (and you will know since you the Top and are monitoring her closely) roll her onto her side. It will save both of you a situation that can quickly go from wonderful to "oh, shit!"

Places Not to Put Your Rope

- The neck
- Over the joints, particularly the notch of the elbow
- Nose and mouth
- Armpits
- Diaphragm (this one is debatable; make sure if there is a tie here it is not a constricting tie).

I'll say it again: play should be fun, but safety should be serious. If you are getting into rope bondage, I urge you to take some hands-on classes. The rope bondage scene has expanded immensely over the years and there are some really interesting and amazing things happening as it grows in the U.S. and around the world. There is no substitute for hands-on learning from those who are more experienced. Go out, buy some of the books that focus on bondage and safety, and then get some hands-on time and have fun.

An old-fashioned quickie really perks up an afternoon. Leave your panties in his pocket after you send him back to work.

Heat Me Up, Baby: Hot Wax

Hot wax for kinky fun is a classic icon—in a steamy Hollywood sex scene you inevitably see a dripping candle being used by the temptress to turn on and slowly torment the lover who is tied to the bed. What makes hot wax so special is, well, it's hot—hot and steamy and also hot to the touch. Watching your lover squirm under your administrations, hearing her breath sucked sharply between her teeth as each drip meets her skin in a pinprick of heat, coating her nipples and tracing an arch down over her belly, closer and closer teasingly to her privates, is something you really have to experience firsthand. Done right it can be an immense turn on; if done wrong it can burn very badly. Many people use a Crock-Pot with wax melting in it for wax play; I'm going to concentrate here on candles since they are the easiest and most available on a Friday night when you are running around picking up supplies for your night of debauchery.

There are a number of different types of wax with differing melting temperatures. It is important to know each one to ensure your submissive's safety when playing with wax—there's nothing sexy about a bad burn.

Type of Wax	Melting Point Range (°F)
■ Religious candles in glass jars (low-temperature wax)	125-132 degrees
■ Paraffin	124-145 degrees
■ Pillar candle	135-141 degrees
■ Beeswax candle	140-160 degrees
■ No-drip, plastic-coated and anything with glitter in it	Too hot

As you can see the glass jar candles that you typically find in religious stores have a much lower melting point and are safer than a beeswax candle, which is at the upper end of the spectrum. The added bonus of the glass jar candles is that they are cool enough to hold in your hand, provided you keep your hand on the body of the votive, below where the candle is burning. I don't use beeswax candles for play since they burn too hot for my liking and I want to be able to continue a scene without having to tend to a second-degree burn on my partner that puts an end to play-time for the weekend. From my own research, the color of the candles doesn't appear to affect the temperature of the wax's melting point, however different scents will raise the melting point approx five degrees. I like the contrast of a nice fresh vanilla scent filling the air while I'm doing some terribly delicious things to my partner, and I adjust my delivery to accommodate the higher temperature. As with everything in kinky sex, use your best judgment.

Typically we use two different types of candles—a tapered or a votive.

Pros of the tapered candle:

■ The wax doesn't have an area to pool so it burns hotter.

■ It gives you greater control at dripping only a little bit at a time.

Pros of the votive candle:

■ The pooling wax is held at a slightly lower temperature than with the taper.

■ It gives you more wax to drip in a line down your lover's body.

So you have your candles and you are ready to turn your submissive into a wax-coated sex puppy, begging and pleading simultaneously for you to stop and give him more. How do we get there? The first thing you need to do is take a little time to test it out on yourself before your play partner even comes over. Typically you can light the candle and drip some wax on yourself from approximately the distance you will have him or her from you. This could be as close as dripping it onto your forearm or onto the

Tell your partner what really turns you on and explore together. If you want to be spanked till you are red and raw, let him/her know!

Facing Page: Neon hot wax candles become really vibrant under black light.

That's a good little pet.

Hot wax play with fluorescent candles under a black light looks spectacular.

top of your foot. Everyone's pain tolerance is slightly different, but this will give you a ballpark idea. Areas that will be more sensitive to the hot wax and you should proceed with more caution are:

- Inner thighs
- Genitals
- Nipples
- That sexy part where the hip and belly meet.

Get your partner naked. Wax on cotton clothing will ruin it and wax on polyester lingerie will ruin the person underneath by melting it to his or her skin. Smooth some baby oil across her body as a way to make for easier removal. The baby oil will stop the wax from sticking as firmly to the skin and to body hair. Having to peel your partner like a banana will pretty much kill the mood if the wax is stuck in her hair and needs to be tugged off. Warm up your partner by starting in a less sensitive area like the shoulders or back and then move toward the more sensitive areas. Take your time, build up the layers and create your own human sculpture

When you peel the wax off, make it slow and sensual, it feels better that way.

with him at the epicenter of the sexual safari. Layering creates a conflicting sensation—on one hand it offers a shield against the initial stinging drips, but the layering also builds up the heat across the area. This isn't a big problem, just another area you want to monitor and if it is becoming too hot for the submissive, introduce some ice cubes to the area to give him a new sensation and to also cool him down. This push and pull of sensations between fire and ice will keep her squirming nicely through your scene. Don't forget to put an old blanket down before you start playing with hot wax. I have one in my home that I use for wax play specifically— one I don't mind that I will never get it clean. It is softer than a tarp and while the slave is writhing on the floor, it gives her more padding underneath to squirm around on.

When dripping wax onto your slave, you can control the temperature at which it hits the submissive by two ways: height and degree of tilt. Dropping it from a height of five feet down onto them on the floor gives the drop a marginal time to cool before it hits them. The other way that I find is more successful comes from a friend of mine named Spectrum, who wrote *The Hot Wax and Temperature Play Toy Bag Book* a few years ago. His method is to tilt the candle 10 degrees so the wax drips down the side approx an inch before dropping down onto your partner. This will help cool it to a tolerable temperature. The longer the drip down the side, the more it can cool. If the wax gets too hot or uncomfortable, have a cold wet towel lying in the bathtub nearby to lay across them if they need to be cooled down immediately. Speak to them in calm reassuring tones. You don't need a fire extinguisher, but remember—safety is your responsibility and you need to set the pace that is manageable by you. Don't rush into the scene no matter how horny you are. Take your time; slow is easier to manage, rather than having to solve a lot of problems because you rushed and you now have an upset and burned submissive on your hands.

Lastly, you'll find out that removing the wax can be just as fun as putting it on them! I like to use a big scary hunting knife with the edge dulled to slide carefully and slowly under the edge of the wax and scrape it off the skin. Be sure to take the edge off the knife so there is minimal chance of cutting them and go slowly, with a firm grip on the handle. If you are not ready for knives yet, your fingernails picking the edges and lifting the wax off in small sheets against the hypersensitive skin will really excite your slave!

Use lots of lube for anal sex and warm up by stroking the outer anus slowly and taking your time. Try a DP (double penetration) with toys for an intense orgasm.

The Play's the Thing: Play/Dungeon Monitors

When you become active and start going to fetish nights, and after demonstrating that you are a person of integrity and well balanced in general, you will more than likely be approached by the organizers of an event to volunteer for a shift as the Play Monitor (PM) or Dungeon Monitor (DM) at a party. This is a wonderful opportunity to be involved with the organizers and get to know people in the fetish world better and it has the altruistic reward of contributing to the community. You will better understand what goes into the organizing of an event and have a larger perspective on it as a whole, and there is no better way to get involved in the beginning. There are safety issues that a PM or DM has to be aware of not only in the physical sense but also in the emotional and mental sense of walking a fine

Good quality latex cat suits come in a wide variety of colors.

When you are having rough sex, use the word "fucker" after "deeper and harder."

line between the venue restrictions, the organizers' rules, and monitoring the play space for safety and ensuring that the players aren't intruded upon. Oh, and you have to make sure that the equipment isn't hogged and that it's cleaned appropriately afterward. You're also charged with ensuring the safety of the patrons and helping the organizer stay on top of potential issues that might end the party early for everyone. It isn't an easy job and more than likely someone at the party is going to bitch later on either about how they didn't get enough time on the equipment or their scene was interrupted, but you can only do your best.

Patrons need to remember that they are guests at a party and house rules are to be respected. All players going into a group party should read and familiarize themselves with the rules beforehand. That said, there are some overzealous PM/DMs who feel their word is law and they have the right to be jerks with a capital J because a scene they are observing goes against their personal interests. I have seen DMs at events intrude and stop a scene that was well within the boundaries of the house rules, merely because the theme squicked their particular sensibilities. Their job is not to personally police a scene and micromanage it but to help the players stay

That's right, do everything the nice lady tells you.

When spanking your partner, change your hand shape from flat to palm cupped and arched to change the sensation. Pull his/her hair too!

within the house rules and more importantly, keep other patrons from stumbling into the play space. This means that they should have first-aid training in case it is needed and a full understanding that the venue rules may or may go beyond their own personal boundaries. As a PM/DM, you are there to help add ambience to the evening and help things run smoothly, and to assist in the event something goes sideways, not to provide homeland security or judgment. Oftentimes a scene will be performed by two or more people and will be outside the area of expertise or experience of the DM. What a DM shouldn't do is interrupt midscene and order the participants to stop with statements like, "You are playing too hard, and I am not comfortable with it." If the house rules are being followed and they are experienced players with their own track record, the DM's comfort level is not important. The host of the party is responsible for adequately training a new PM/DM; that is one of their jobs—they should not assume the PM/DM is familiar with all the house rules. Typically an organizer or host will ask the monitors for that evening to show up a half hour before the event for a briefing on equipment and safety procedures, to ensure the evening flows smoothly. As a PM/DM new to the community, if there is an issue you are not comfortable with, you should find the host of the party and ask him or her how they want to proceed, since it is the host that is ultimately responsible.

I was playing at a party a while ago where the submissive I was suspending had his hands turn purple in the bondage, something that would normally be a cause of concern to those of us who want the play to be safe, right? The well-meaning but misguided PM/DM interrupted my scene and demanded that the submissive be lowered immediately. Let me restate the point I made above—the PM/DMs are not there to police a scene. I am a very accomplished bondage rigger and player and with this particular submissive, who I have suspended and tied up many times in the past, I knew the limits of his body and knew that no matter how lightly you tied him, his body's response to any bondage was always to turn his fingers light purple. He is very aware of his body, practices yoga, works out and is in top physical health and most of all we communicate and we trust each other. He is an excellent partner because he monitors his own body and space as the scene progresses and has no problem with keeping me apprised of the situation

Facing Page: Thigh-high boots never go out of fashion.

If you are an exhibitionist, turn yourself in the passenger seat of the car, hike up your skirt and masturbate for him.

as the scene unravels. Subsequently I found the host of the event and explained what had happened and he took matters into his own hands to rectify the problem with the PM/DM. Of course all the energy of my scene was lost and a great play session was wasted because of a misguided PM/DM. The DM is there to serve and assist the host. When in doubt, if you are a PM/DM, and there is no glaring safety issue, always defer to the host. A PM/DM or party attendee can ruin a party simply by not understanding what is happening in a scene that may be out of his or her range of experience. If you are going to play hard at a party or do something particularly intense, let the host know ahead of time (usually at the beginning of the party when things are still relatively quiet) and ask for feedback and whether or not they are comfortable with your plans. There is nothing more frustrating than clearing a takedown scene with the host and then having a misguided DM/PM jumped into the pile with the rest of the players. What might be a carefully choreographed scene could become dangerous with an additional person pushing and shoving, not knowing that all the players are accustomed to their roles. Necks can get twisted, arms and fingers could get stepped on and what started out as a fun struggle scene now results in sprains and icing the injured parts because of a PM/DM that simply "didn't know." If you are doing DM shift, always ask the host if there is something unusual preplanned for that night and ask for direction, for the sake of the venue, the hosts, the patrons and your own safety.

Take My Breath Away: Choking and Breath Play

In a nutshell, don't do it. I know you have probably seen some great things online or read hot fantasies or even tried choking in bed, but the risks that are inherent in cutting off the air supply to your partner are not worth it. Let me just give you a quick example of how important air is—the first thing a paramedic or anyone who is administering first aid does is check to see if the injured person is breathing. There will be people who tell you that they can do it "safely," and people who want to have it done to them; on Internet forums you will find people discussing judo chokes and how to apply them to your sex life—it is a hot and sexy and fascinating idea, but call me old fashioned or overly cautious: I don't want any of my scenes that might go sideways to involve a visit from the police and coroner's office. It is tough enough to explain the hooks in your ceiling to your

There are many sexier—and safer—ways to play with sensory deprivation than choking or breath play.

mom, how will you explain that you took a breath play workshop and thought you would give it a go and now your partner is either dead or brain damaged? Sorry, but I just can't get behind people on this one as a good idea for playtime. I am sure I am going to get mail from people who engage in it, but for me there is too much cost for not enough of a pleasurable return. Make your own choices as a responsible adult but my personal stance is very firm on this one.

Five Key Points to Remember about Playing Safe:

- If a scene goes sideways, don't panic. Calm action will save the day.
- Nothing is perfectly safe, but safety is your responsibility for what and whom you play with.
- Arnica cream can help heal bruises.
- Start hot wax play with the low-temperature religious candles in the tall jars.
- PM/DMs are not there to police your scene at a public event; it is your job to stay within the boundaries of the venue rules.

Chapter Eight

Developing in Your Community

A mediocre Master tells, a good Master teaches, an excellent Master explains, but a true Master inspires.
—Anonymous

In my first book, I encouraged readers to find their local scene, attend munches, seek out play parties and get connected with a larger social network of real-life experiences rather than cloistering themselves online. In this chapter we are going to look more closely at developing within your kinky community, and ways in which you may also contribute to the scene in a positive and meaningful way.

Like-Minded Gatherings: Munches

If you are reading this book, I am going to assume you have been to a munch or sought one out. Munches are a great way to meet people in the scene and get your feet wet without encountering the expectations or conventions of a fetish party. Perhaps you live in a small town where there don't appear to be any regular munches; what can you do? The Internet has connected us in so many ways, but sometimes there are real-life limitations on what we can do or what resources are available. If you are in this position, or just

Facing Page: This ass will be sore in the morning!

When giving him a blow job, pause to ask him where he wants to shoot his load on you.

find that there isn't an established munch that appeals to you—I encourage you to start your own. Munches aren't hard to organize; with the social networking sites available now like Fetlife, as well as local lists on Yahoo groups, you can easily create a time and place for like-minded people to consistently meet once a month. Expect a slow start: years ago, when I first established the munch for Canadian Equus, which eventually turned out to be Canada's largest pony play group, my munch began with exactly two people, one of them me. Me and a donkey boy who I still admire to this day, sitting in a coffee shop sharing stories and ideas about what we liked so much about pony play. It was a cold, windswept night in a little town north of Toronto in horse country (naturally). The country road on which Tim Horton's coffee shop sat was as lonely as the dark sky outside. Donkey boy and I shared ideas, spoke frankly about what we wanted to try to put together and came up with a framework for the group over hot tea and scones in a few hours. Neither of us knew many people who were into pony play but we had faith that there were others out there. We'd seen the odd sex documentary or book at one of the local sex shops, and there was a wonderful magazine called *Equus Eroticus* run by Paul and Emily Reed that fueled our desires. We decided that we would run a munch once a month in Toronto and see who showed up. I posted on a local Yahoo group and we booked time at a great pub downtown with shiny brass rails, dark oak furniture and a crackling fireplace and crossed our fingers and hoped people would come. As we sat there, we wondered what we would do if no one came. What could be the worst that would happen? We figured that if worse came to worse, we would sit for an afternoon just the two of us and have a few pints and chat about kinky things. But people did show up; people who were curious, and we tripled our number for our first munch downtown, six people. More importantly, we got some positive feedback on the lists. The next month more people showed up and then the next month more and even more the third month. By the time summer arrived we had enough people to take over a whole section of the pub, and we were ready to run our first pony play event on a private farm resplendent with a barn and obstacle course. As an added bonus, Paul and Emily heard about it and they came to do the judging; we had a great event with lots of food and fun on a beautiful summer day amongst the rolling limestone hills.

That was my lesson: if you organize and offer something on an angle or topic that isn't being offered otherwise, people will come. Word of

A look of terror on the face of their slave makes every mistress hot.

When he gets ready to cum, pull down firmly but gently on his ball sack to delay his orgasm until YOU are ready for him to cum.

mouth spreads fast in the scene, but not as fast as a posting on a social networking site. Here are some tips and ideas that will help you with setting up your first munch:

1. Find a venue that is kink friendly. Bear in mind that a munch shouldn't involve any play or showing off in kink gear or toys. We want to keep the vanilla people in the bar unaware of the subject matter since it really isn't any of their business anyway. Call a few pubs and ask if they have a side room that you can arrange to use for a group meeting; tell them that this is for people that belong to a group that discusses alternative sexuality to just come and relax and chill. Don't be evasive—the bar has a right to know what your group does; they just don't need to know the details. This gives the manager the opportunity to put servers on your room who would be comfortable with your group, rather than someone who might freak out at the talk of whips or the pleasures of clothespins on nipples.

2. Come up with a snappy name, but not a stupid one. "Tracey's Top Tuesday at the Tulip Lounge" pretty much conveys what the munch is about, what night it is on and where it is. You can also go with something more low key like "The Orlando Meet-Up Group" if you want to keep things even more under the radar. This really depends on how receptive your venue is. Keep in mind one thing about bars or restaurants like Denny's—you are asking a manager if you can bring a group of paying customers into his or her establishment to sit, eat, drink and socialize for a few hours. These places are in business for a reason, and if you schedule your event in the middle of the week when things might be slow for the venue, they will usually be very receptive.

3. When you post it on the list, tell people to walk in and just ask for "Tracey's Tuesday Group." That way they are discrete in asking. The munch organizer will let you know how to ask for the group if you have contacted them earlier.

4. Create some guidelines and rules. If you are going to be the creator and organizer of the munch, you have to make yourself responsible for interacting with the staff of the bar or restaurant and your group members,

Facing Page: Good pets get treats!

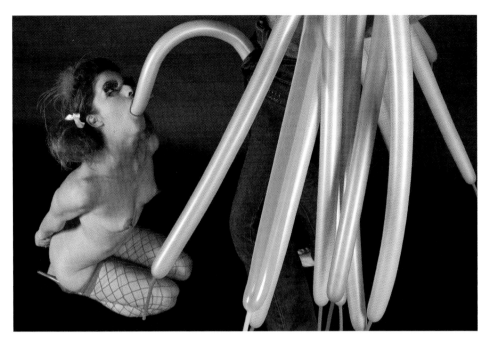

Sharing your kink with others can give you the confidence to explore even further.

should there be a problem. If you allow people to get out of control it will reflect badly on you. We are not aiming to ram our lifestyle or interests down others' throats. Running a munch requires you to be an ambassador; conduct yourself as one. Typical guidelines for a much could be as simple as a) no toys or fetish wear; b) keep the conversations respectful; c) be sensitive to the vanillas that might be around and be welcoming if they express interest; d) No play of any kind; e) no nudity and f) what is discussed at the munch stays at the munch. There are lots of sample rules available online; glean from them what suits you best.

Push a pair of ice cubes into her and then take her for a walk while they melt and drip down her legs in public.

5. Make sure the servers know that everyone will be on separate bills! Don't let yourself or someone else get stuck with the tab.

6. Set a time limit, maybe three hours. Some munches are run in the late afternoon on a fetish night so people can meet up and socialize before the event later on; other munches are in the middle of the week, which offers a nice respite from a dreary work week.

Facing Page: Whatever your particular kink, others will be into it too!

Come closer, I bite!

Above all else, try to keep it fun and enjoyable. Being a munch organizer requires you to be a secretary, organizer and den mother all in one. It is a great way to give others an idea of your interests and to meet new people.

Human beings have a natural desire to be part of a community and to surround themselves with others who share their interests, values and drives. Kinky people want to hang out with other kinky people, and if a community doesn't already exist then they'll start working to create and build one. There's also the "newbie" factor: munches are usually the first point of contact for people exploring their kinky side (at least, after the Internet). Those new people bring a fresh perspective to things and help to keep the kinky community vibrant, dynamic and ever changing.

There's satisfaction in having helped build something that has had a lasting effect on the lives of others. Over the years I've seen countless people enter the community, and begin making discoveries about themselves and their own desires. I've seen them explore, and grow, and develop. I've seen them form lasting relationships. I've seen them laugh, and cry, and fall in love. I've seen them reach the heights of ecstasy, as well as find the quiet comfort of being surrounded by others like themselves. Knowing that my efforts have helped create an atmosphere in which all of those things are possible is enormously satisfying.

—Bernie, Eh.B.C., Canada's longest-running BDSM support group

Make them wear your collar and leash and attach it to the headboard before they go to sleep.

Following the Leader: Mentorship

Mentorship is a frequent topic in the kink world. What's the point of having a mentor when there is a plethora of books and Internet articles that you can glean information from? Books and online material are great resources; they come packed full of all kinds of information that can be very valuable—but there is something irreplaceable about learning one on one with a mentor you can look up to, someone in real time who can answer your questions and show you techniques that a YouTube video just cannot convey. How do you find a mentor and how exactly can a mentor help with your kinky explorations?

A mentor should have walked your path before: a submissive or slave should seek out a submissive or slave mentor, a Dominant should seek out a Master. It is a teacher/student relationship. Mentors should not only be masters in their subject, but patient, supportive, respected, people oriented

Having a good mentor can take you places you never thought you'd end up!

and *effective teachers*. That last one is key. Many people are natural superstars in the scene with flogging, whips, fireplay, aural seduction and so on, but unless they can convey the specific skills that make them "superstars"— show another how to dissect and approach their style or technical skill— then they won't be able to pass it on effectively. Most mentors I know are quiet and thoughtful. They are not always the biggest, baddest Domme in the room. They listen to questions carefully and then give a complete answer. They assess your skill level and decide where you can go in your next step. Unfortunately some of the best mentors are so good that their time is limited and it is hard to find one that is willing to take on a student.

A mentorship should never be sexual in nature. If your "mentor" wants to get in bed with you and you're game, then go right ahead—but then find yourself another mentor because a sexual dynamic will compromise the educational aspect. It always does. This situation should not be confused with a partner/friend/fuckbuddy/play partner dynamic where you are learning and sharing with each other; people will always exchange idea and techniques. I am referring to a very specific learning model known as mentorship. Good mentors are a wonderful resource and if you learn your own skill set properly and with sincerity with the guidance of a mentor, you may find yourself ready to take on a protégé of your own in a few years. Really great mentors are also people who understand that no matter how advanced they are, they are committed to lifelong learning themselves, constantly sharpening their skills and refining their own BDSM practices.

> When role-playing as Little Red Riding Hood, make sure the Big Bad Wolf eats you (out), just like the story says.

Finding a Mentor: Where to Look

As you gain access to the community, take time to get to know the people that are most established and see what they have to offer in their particular area of expertise. I recommend asking them, politely, three to five specific questions when exploring whether they would be interested in becoming your mentor. For example:

■ Who mentored you or where did you learn?

■ How would you approach a particular situation of personality clashes between a Dominant and submisive?

■ What do you believe to be the best qualities of a Master or a slave?

■ What would mentorship look like to us?

These kinds of questions will give you an idea of their methodology.

If you are going to try fisting, make sure you are both horny as hell and then use tons of lube. Go slow and steady and concentrate on breathing and relaxing.

Then if you think it is a good match, you can politely ask if they would consider taking you on to help you develop your skills. What I don't encourage is depending only on an online mentorship—you need to get offline and into the real world. A mentorship can be part time in nature; given the demands that life puts on us, sometimes that is all it can be. People online can claim to be anything you want them to be; find a mentor in the real world, with a reputation for conducting him or herself in an honest, straightforward manner. Later on, once a mentorship relationship has been established, the Internet can be a valuable tool for keeping linked. Is it possible to have more than one mentor at a time? Yes, provided they know about each other and the information they are giving you isn't contradictory.

Depending on the nature of your relationship to your mentor and factoring in issues of time and proximity, he or she will probably be able to put you in touch with other people and resources that will help you develop and learn. A mentor should be encouraging of you developing a varied skill set, and he or she should not be threatened by other sources of learning. If your mentor says any of the following, you might want to reconsider the relationship:

- *I am one of the TRUE lifestylers in the scene.*
- *I have been around since the beginning and know everything.*
- *No one is as good as me.*
- *It's okay, I learned all this from a master in Europe, we msn all the time!*

A really good mentor should embody all of the values that you admire and never stop his or her own learning process.

Helping Them Find Their Footing: How to Be a Good Mentor

There will come a time when you have refined your own practice and gained sufficient skills that you feel you are ready to take on a protégé. How do you know you are ready to be a mentor and how do you structure your teaching so that a protégé can take advantage of your knowledge and learn on his or her own in the process? My personal experience in being a mentor focuses on one person per year. I believe that any more than that

Facing Page: You should choose a mentor who embodies traits that you admire and carries themselves with grace and confidence.

A good mentor will find out what you're interested in and help you find yourself within that realm.

Be uncomplicated but not easy.

will mean spreading yourself too thin. Online you will see people who have lots of designations, like "In a house with a relationship, mentoring, training and topping submissive/pet CandiGrrl." That sounds like way too much work to me and way too many hats. I prefer a simpler public approach to my mentorship that is based on my experience as a professionally trained educator. Online isn't as important as real-life experiences where you can talk, discuss, interact, watch and learn from someone who has been down the same path as yourself, just earlier.

As a mentor you should be respectful and polite and encouraging as you share your knowledge, but you should also allow for the relationship to be dynamic. No doubt your protégé will suggest new and improved ways of doing things you have demonstrated; don't take this as an attempt to one-up you—encourage him to explore and expand his knowledge, but also be ready to offer feedback on what he is doing, how it might be improved or whether or not it is potentially unsafe. Your protégé needs for you to be straightforward and honest in your encouragement and assessment of her ideas and performance. You should offer challenging feedback sandwiched between positive reinforcement—the Oreo method described in *How to Be*

Always do as you're told...

Because it sticks only to itself, bondage tape is absolutely perfect for trying out new positions.

Kinky: A Beginner's Guide to BDSM. There is no reason someone has to reinvent the wheel, but there is also no law against using that "wheel" to their advantage. Once I demonstrated how to do a specific type of Japanese bondage harness called a box tie for my protégé. She took that knowledge, practiced it over and over and a month later at a rope group meeting showed me how she had improved on the traditional tie with her own flair. I see my role as that of a guide and facilitator, and you should too.

I formally work with one person a year to help them find their path as a Dominant or Master/Mistress, a dynamic that works best for my personality and allows me to give my protégé the attention he or she deserves. It's gratifying to me when their own skill sets eventually outshine mine and they go on to bigger opportunities. If you are a great mentor and teacher, the student should eventually outshine you. This is the biggest compliment that they can pay you. Your time in someone's life can be as long or as fleeting as both of you like; what lasts are the lessons taught with sincerity and respect. As a mentor, you will have feelings and emotions too, but if your protégé goes on to be a bright superstar in the scene, remember that he or she did it in part because of your influence and you should be encouraging, provided they reached their position respectfully and with good old-fashioned hard work. The biggest part of being a mentor is the ability to take a large skill and break it down into a series of manageable steps, be it hard or soft skills—more on those in a moment.

Following Respectfully: Being a Good Protégé

I can't discuss mentorship without also talking about the flip side—being the protégé. It is natural that you are eager and ready to learn everything you can from your mentor but you don't want to be annoying. How do you strike a balance between asking thoughtful questions and behaving like a yappy dog at someone's heels? You need to be able to be respectful and polite. Anyone worth being a mentor will let you know exactly how much time he or she will have available for helping you develop. A mentor will take the time to let you know where the boundaries are—specifically at a fetish night. You might be invited to shadow him at an event, either to assist or just to watch.

Facing Page: The skills you will learn as a protégé will keep your kink life fulfilling and exciting for years to come.

How to make a double wide ball gag

1 This is a very easy gag to make. All you need is a piece of dowel, two ball gags and some wide ribbons. **2** For the side-by-side position, loop some sexy ribbon over the end, around the back of the first submissive's head and then to the middle. **3** Go around the back of the head of the second submissive and then split the ribbon around the wooden rod. **4** You don't need to over-wrap the ribbon. Tying it off at the end is a great finish. **5** Make a pretty bow; neatness counts!

6 The facing forward position follows the same wraps, only with their positions being opposite.
7 Wrap the ribbon around the back of the head of one submissive, then up around the wooden
rod... 8 then around the back of the head of the second sexy submissive. 9 Split the ribbon
around the wooden rod and finish with a bow. 10 Ready to go!

If you are attempting fisting for the first time, slow and steady wins the race, rather than treating the prostate like the speedbag in a boxing gym.

What you shouldn't expect is for the mentor to spend his entire evening babysitting you. Be a complement to your mentor as requested and she will in turn help sharpen your skills and approach to the lifestyle. If he has invited you to be a part of a scene so he can do a demonstration in public, don't ever question or criticize his decisions in public unless there is a large breech of safety involved. Ideally if he or she has asked you to be part of a public scene, he will have already discussed the evening ahead of time. You both should have a private time set aside afterward for questions and answers. If you have been given certain responsibilities to perform when assisting him, do so with good will. You will have your own ideas about how to approach playtime or service, and the mentor should encourage you to express and explore them, but if he is demonstrating something specific and has you involved, then it is because he wants you to have a specific foundation upon which to build.

Neither the mentor nor the protégé should ever exhibit anything but a positive manner in public. There may be times when you have conflicting ideas and as a protégé you will have to accept that your mentor might not have the same ideas about how to approach a situation; you must defer to their experience and then take what you can from it, handle it with dignity and grace and remember that respect is a two-way street. Once I had a disagreement with my own mentor regarding a situation where a slave was bad-mouthing her current Master in public at a munch. I felt the slave should have been taken aside in private and made to understand in no uncertain terms that her behavior was unacceptable, whereas my Mentor believed that she should be confronted, aggressively, in public due to her pattern of past behavior. Later on after the munch he shared with me that particular slave had a habit of bouncing from Master to Master whenever a new one came on the scene. She was self absorbed and would bounce to another scene soon enough and that the current Master she was with was too inexperienced to deal with her self-destructive and selfish behavior. I was glad that he and I discussed it later and I saw that as his protégé it wasn't my place to disagree in public but support him and get more of the back story afterward to better shape my own understanding of the scene in that particular city, where I was merely visiting. While my mentor and I have relaxed the teacher/student roles over the past fifteen years, to this day I still consider him a wonderful resource and more importantly, a sounding board as I continually navigate my way along. If you embrace the concept of lifelong learning you will never be without new skill sets to master or to share.

At every conference you will learn something new—then be eager to test it out!

Microbondage on body parts such as the feet can be a fantastic way to shake up your routine a little.

Needle play

Activities like needle play show the possibilities of how much fun and hot more kinky play can be. Play piercing, as it is also called, is used for endorphin release and body decoration. It is considered edge play in the BDSM and Kinky community. These images demonstrate where you can go once you learn how from someone experienced and have obtained the necessary medical training; they are not a substitute for hands-on, real life training. Blood play has a higher risk factor associated with it in regards to blood health related issues and infection and both the top and bottom have to understand and accept that it is an activity with higher risk before engaging in it. It is your responsibility to obtain the proper training before you go get all "stabby" on your partner. Included in your training should include a discussion and understanding of Methicillin-Resistant Staphylococcus Aureus (MSRAs) and other bacterial strains that can cause complications. Forewarned is forearmed.

It is important to know the difference between sterile and clean. The needles and sutures we use come pre packaged and are sterile: meaning that it has gone through a process in an autoclave that has killed any living micro organism on it. It is not a readily available service and you will need to know a Dr. or Vet or a body piercing/tattoo shop or purchase one yourself which are in excess of $500. An oven, boiling water or dishwasher is not a substitute for an autoclave. It is essential that the equipment that punctures the body is sterile. Clean on the other hand means that it has not gone through this process but it is a clean as we can make it. Objects like disposable surgical sheets and gloves are clean but not sterile. We use a combination of both of them in order to reduce the chance of infection. Whether or not they are clean or sterile, these are one-time use only objects and should be disposed of in the proper manner when finished.

Disposable hypodermic needles are thin, cheap, disposable, sterile and best of all come with a plastic cup on one end that the syringe fits into but for what we do with them acts as an ideal handle and prevents them from being pushed all the way through the skin. Needle gauge or diameter is categorized by a descending numerical system and have a colored end that corresponds with its size. The diameter number increases as the thickness decreases. They are also available in a variety of lengths. For this demonstration, we are using a 22 gauge needle that has a blue cap and its length is 1.5 inches. All disposable needle boxes are clearly labeled.

How to do play piercing

1 Have a nicely organized kit where you can see all of your equipment. 2 A disposable surgical sheet will have a plastic backing on it in order to protect the surface from blood and other bio-waste. The clean area that you are preparing to pierce must never come in contact with the sheet or anything other than the sterile equipment and your gloves. 3 Place this plastic backing face down on the area you are working on so that any blood or fluids are caught by the absorbent side which should be facing up, against the person's body. 4 Spread the sheet to cover the entire area you are working on top of. 5 It is important to have a Bio-Hazard Sharps Container to dispose of your needles and sutures.

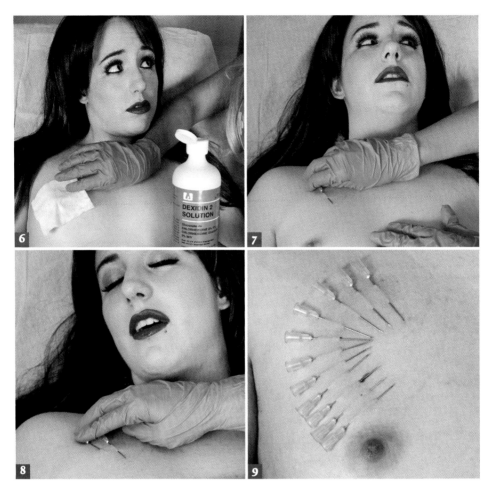

6 Prep the area with an antiseptic solution. We used Dexiden 2, applied from sterile gauze, but a comparable antiseptic is fine. Do not dry the surface; the area does not need to be dry to proceed. Once you are gloved, if you touch anything non sterile—your hair, face, kits, etc—you must re-glove. 7 Now that the area has been cleaned it is time to begin. We have chosen the breast area because it is nice and fleshy. If your submissive isn't already anxious about the needles after preparing the area, they will be once you pierce the skin. You are aiming the needle to just pierce the skin and not the underlying tissue. You don't have to go deep and you will be surprised at how resilient the skin is. A firm steady push that is controlled is how you want to proceed as it enters and then exits the skin. 8 After the first one is in, it gets easier for the submissive. The nervousness and build up to the first one is over and now they can relax and enjoy those endorphins as they start to flush through their body. 9 Add more in a pretty pattern! The first time you do it you will be surprised at the lack of blood. Occasionally you will hit a vein that is close to the surface and that is ok. You can pull it back out and try a different spot. The blood that comes out should be bright cherry red, not dark oxygenated blood.

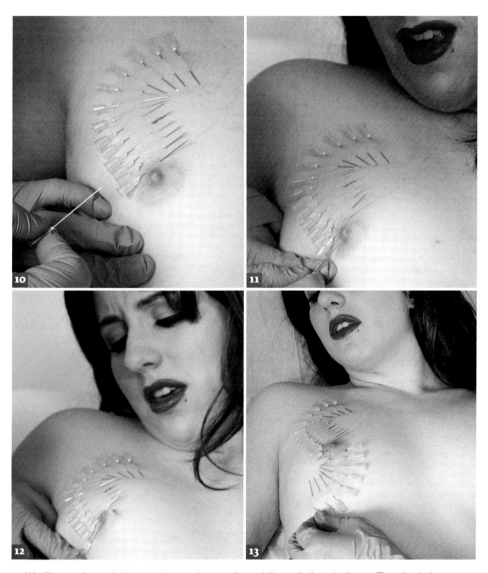

10 We like to pierce right up and onto the areola and through the nipple. 11 The nipple is
extremely resilient and you will need to push harder. Aim the needle at the base of the nipple.
Keep the pressure firm and steady, resist the urge to jab or shove. The submissive will find this a
more painful area than on the broad surfaces of her skin. Encourage them, reassure that you are
proud of them and they are very safe in your care. 12 Your submissive might squeak a little at
this one! Be sure to be very comforting and gentle with your words. 13 After we have pierced
the nipple, we continued the pattern in a clockwise direction. Don't be disappointed if your
submissive can't take more than a few needles on the first play date. Give them time to work up
to it. Breaking the ice for the first time in a controlled and steady manner will give you both a
chance to build trust and work up to a larger number of needles in future playdates.

14 Look at that, we are almost done! If you are feeling more sadistic you can slowly twist or rotate the needle for extra stimulation. Make sure you know your submissive very well before introducing this sensation. 15 What a good girl! Our lovely submissive Lyarah has taken all the needles; she has a nice endorphin flush and is pretty proud of herself. Give your submissive time to enjoy this moment. There is no rush to remove the needles. She might be crying or finishing crying or about to cry. Let her body relax and adjust to these sensations. 16 When it is time to remove the needles, pull the end and let it slide out of the skin. Do NOT try to fit it back into the plastic safety cap it came with. The chances of inadvertently stabbing yourself are high and if you do, you will then have a cross contamination issue to deal with. Instead just grasp the colored cap, pull it out and drop it into a sharps container.

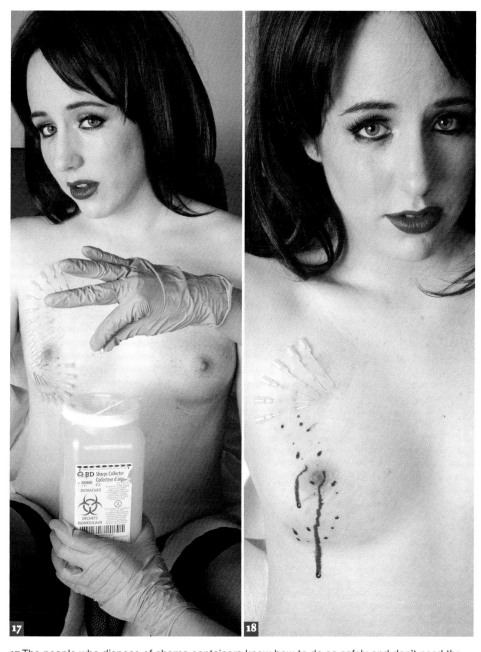

17 The people who dispose of sharps containers know how to do so safely and don't need the safety cap on the needle as the entire container will be incinerated. Find a proper disposal method for your sharps container when it is full. **18** When the needles come out, let the area bleed a bit. It will help flush out the wound. Once the bleeding has stopped you can use a disposable swab to clean away the blood. If you have been successful the piercing should leave a tiny hole that will barely be visible and then disappears in a few days.

If you know that your fingers are going somewhere sensitive, treat yourself to a manicure and tell the technician to smooth down the edges. Sharp nails are great to run down a back but not so welcome when they're pushed in somewhere else.

We like this diameter because it offers more control than the thinner needles and is right in the middle of the pain range. The lower the diameter the thicker the needle and the more skin it has to displace which equals more pain. 22 gauge is a perfect size when first beginning.

Hard and Soft Skill Sets

Skills that your mentor will attempt to share and instill in you can be broken down into either hard or soft skills. Hard skills are tangible—how to use a singletail whip, bondage methods, the use of plastic wrap or hot wax; something that can be demonstrated, learned and encouraged in a physical sense. Soft skills are intangible but no less important than hard skills: the respectful and polite manner that you should use to treat people in the scene, protocol nuances, dependability and conscientiousness, social graces and personal habits. It can be these soft skills that define how you're thought of in the scene, regardless of your skill or talent in your field. For example: once at a fetish party I was doing a spanking demonstration and having a lot of fun doing it. I needed three volunteers, which were quickly found, but I had about five more single submissives volunteer, more than I could handle for the demonstration. The hard skill set I was demonstrating was the spanking techniques but the soft skill set I demonstrated to my protégé was how to take those five eager submissives and politely tell them that I had enough volunteers for my demo but if they were interested in being volunteers for the hands-on portion for some of the extra single people at the class, that would be terrific. I would be there watching and helping the Tops learn how to spank them but I definitely had enough for my demonstration portion of the evening. That way I didn't reject them; no one likes rejection, especially if they are volunteering, but I was still was able to keep them involved and make them feel that their eagerness and contribution was valued by me. Afterward I made sure I thanked each one individually in a friendly and respectful way. Both your hard and soft skill sets are what will set you apart from others in the scene. It is how people will discuss your techniques and also your manners. I like to set extremely high expectations for myself, much higher than others would have for me, so I always keep reaching to be the best I can be. It takes time, discipline, empathy and a willingness to share your skills with others that will help you grow in your kinky practice.

Be gentle both physically and mentally when introducing something new—especially if it's the lollipop prostate massage wand!

Fetish and Lifestyle Conferences

What happens at these and what is the point of going to them? Are they worth your time and effort even if you have already found a mentor and explored your local scene?

Ideally you should be using all resources available for learning opportunities. But a Fetish or Lifestyle conference offers something more than intangible words and concepts read on the Internet or the careful tutelage from someone more experienced than you. It is the chance to meet, network and exchange ideas and skills with others who are just as deviant as you; hundreds of them. These conferences typically bring people internationally together. Events such as Shibaricon, Floating World, Mr. Leather Toronto, Thunder in the Mountains, International Mister Leather and South Plains Leatherfest, to name a few, are all conferences that will help you to network and explore how others do things similarly and differently than you do. In all the years I have been teaching at or attending conferences, I have never gone to any conference and *not* come away with a new technique or a new way to approach playtime, or some new mental treat to gnaw on and wonder over when I get home.

Pitfalls of Learning

When you go to these conferences, you will more than likely see some really tasty technique, perhaps a new approach that you think can enhance the protocol with your slave and you want to introduce it into your relationship, but are hesitant as to how to do so successfully. There is a lot to absorb from conferences and sometimes we come away with the kid in a candy store response: so much to try, how do we know what to start with and how do we know that it is going to compliment rather than complicate our relationship dynamic?

Like any relationship, D/s relationships need communication and clarity, plus consistency. It is one thing to want to implement something new; it can be an entirely different challenge to do so successfully. It isn't just up to the Dominant or Top to manage the new challenge; it requires work from both or all the people in the relationship to navigate it successfully. Keep in mind that conferences with all their attendees are just a snapshot

Voice training is a great way to keep your presence on your slave; make sure he knows which phrases he should use to address others even when you are not there.

Facing Page: Knives can be thrilling in the right hands!

251

An enticing outfit can make every scene hotter and make your Bottom submit to your every desire!

of the lifestyle and the promise it holds for happy and satisfying relationships. It is one thing to see a superhot protocol class, led by the Grand Poobah of the house of Thor's Iron Fist, but when you get home and try to implement the same style of protocol, you and your partner may feel let down when it doesn't run as smoothly or fluidly as you saw it working at the conference. You may wonder what went wrong and why you both couldn't make it "work" like you saw it at the conference. This usually leads to feelings of frustration for both the Top and bottom. Relax: it's normal for things to not run exactly like you saw them demonstrated.

Often what works best is to reduce what you want to take from a new technique or activity down to its essence and then shift and change it to suit your own style and lifestyle opportunities. Take from the workshop an element you think would work really well for you both. Find the nugget of gold within someone else's information and take from it what works for you. It is okay not to use everything you saw.

For those who are into public demonstrative of service, for example, someone might have his or her slave pick them up at the airport after a business trip and then kneel in the arrivals terminal to kiss their boots; others might find that too public and prefer to wait until they get to the hotel before the boot licking begins. Choose what is right for you and your lives together and don't measure your success against others. There are realities of that situation that might not sit well with your own boundaries. What if there are families in the terminal that might be uncomfortable with such a display of affection? These are questions you need to ask yourself about what is important and what is appropriate in a given situation that only you can sort out in your life. I like to take the best parts from workshops and demonstrations I see and think of it as rebuilding a car—I leave the engine that drives and provides movement intact but change the body and appearance to suit my own style, keeping what is important and what works for my life in public and in private. There are no rules for BDSM, much to many people's dismay, but there are conventions and you will be surprised, once you start paying attention to the little details in your kinky practice, how much you can recognize those details in others in the vanilla world. It might be how one person carries another's bags in the shopping mall; it might be how one lover wraps his fingers around the neck of his loved one as they walk down the street, or even how doors magically open for another due to the efforts of some lucky submissive. The details are

> When you and your partner move further into BDSM, watch kinky porn together to find out what turns her on without asking direct questions.

Chains can leave telltale marks on the neck and wrists so everyone knows what your slave has been doing!

Mirrors can bring a whole new dimension to a scene or bedroom.

there; it's fun to watch and figure out who is who and what they are into just from the little actions that unfold under the noses of the vanilla world.

When you are ready to introduce something new into your relationship, be it a new technique or protocol, here are a few tips to help smooth the way and give this new practice the opportunity to either flourish or flounder. Dominants, understand that submissives or bottoms don't deal well with sudden changes in behavior or erratic whims. They like consistency and sometimes react unfavorably and challenge new rules or desires if they don't "like it" or can't figure out why it is you want to change things. Taking your submissive's feelings into account and explaining why you want to change or introduce something new will go a long way to reassuring the submissive or bottom that you are taking both your best interests to heart. Bottoms and submissives do well with structure because of the hierarchy that BDSM and kinky sex has at its fundamental core. When something new challenges that, or worse, doesn't even remotely fit in with the structure you have created, it can cause them to question other decisions you have made in the past or

There's a good boy. Do as mistress tells you!

There's nothing better than a fierce boy with a flogger!

other structures you have in place. Communication is beneficial to everyone when introducing something new, and sometimes your partner may not like this new element at first, but he or she should try to understand it and why you want to introduce it and how it is going to benefit your relationship. Submissives have an inborn need to please and Dominants have a need to be served and if both or all parties can get on board the same kinky communication train, the better chance for success everyone is going to have.

Dominants

- You need your submissive to understand why you are implementing something new and the reasoning behind it
- You need them to be willing to give it 100 percent for a trial period
- You need them to trust to follow your lead
- You need to be consistent

Submissives

■ You deserve to know why your Dominant is introducing or implementing something new

■ You are required to give it 100 percent for the trial period

■ You don't have to follow blindly, but you should be willing to surrender and not unconsciously sabotage the activity

■ You deserve consistency when something new is introduced

Success, like failure, is something that both partners are responsible for. This is a dynamic made up of people and people will stumble at times. We all do. How we pick ourselves back up and arrange the pieces into a more manageable order is the mark of reputable character regardless of whether you are a Mistress or a slave. Not everyone has all the answers. Sometimes the only way you can judge whether or not something is going to be successful is by trying it out and learning from what goes right and what doesn't go right. When you are in a loving D/s relationship, you need to be able to say, "Yep, that didn't work out very well, but now we know because we gave 100 percent of our energy toward trying it." This is much better than the "Just do it because I tell you to"—which typically leads to resentment. Likewise, if something is successful, it is because you both found what was important and managed to incorporate it in your activities because you both find value in it. The difference between a satisfying real-life relationship and one based in fantasy is keeping those lines of communication open and having a healthy dose of empathy for one another. Take care of those that take care of you and you will be able to weather anything in your relationship

If you are interested in needle play, visit your local dungeon for demonstrations on temporary play piercing.

Five Key Points for Developing in Your Community:

■ Running a munch is a good way to expand your community and give back to it

■ A mentor should have walked the same path as you

■ Conferences are a great place to meet and share new ideas

■ Consistency and empathy are key points when introducing something new

■ You and your partner(s) are all responsible for success and failure in the relationship

Chapter Nine

How to Be a Pro: Finding Your Niche

The few who do are the envy of the many who only watch.

—Jim Rohn

How do you become influential in the kinky community? Can you make a living as a fetish model? And how do you juggle all the logistics involved in event organizing? Let's look at this last aspect first.

Organizing Events

As we saw in the previous chapter, organizing munches is a lot of work but well worth the effort. Once you get the munch organizing under your belt, you will most likely want to try putting on a kink event. Organizing an event takes a lot of work. Be prepared to prove that "the host works the most." Most people organize events out of a love for the group. When you take charge of putting together an event, you will receive accolades from lots of people in the community and, unfortunately, you will likely be subject to criticism from those who do not step up to organize events themselves. You may find that those who do the least in the community typically whine the loudest. It's just as true with our scene as with other

Facing Page: Face and head bondage are easy and fun and only require a bit of yarn.

organizations that aren't even kink related. How many times have you been in a meeting at work and the person complaining the loudest is the person who does the least? To deal with those people, the best defense is to steadily build your reputation for organizing fun, safe and consensual parties. If you do a good job you will have backup from people who love your parties. Don't be swayed by negative feedback from only a few people. If the overwhelming majority of people are positive, then take their comments and energy and help it to shape your next event. Be focused about what you want to do for your event: do you want it to be educational, informative, political, play based or a something else?

Fantasies are hot but keep a foot in reality; recognize your boundaries when you reach them.

Here is what you will need to do:

1. Find a venue (that has appropriate insurance)
2. Find a crowd (or audience)
3. Arrange the entertainment and volunteers
4. Get a website together and promote it
5. Send out invites to existing mailing lists—be polite to other organizers and demonstrate that you are not competing with them
6. Create promotional print material and plan for effective distribution
7. Arrange for play equipment to be delivered or go fetch it yourself
8. Work your ass off on the evening of the event and be REALLY good at delegation (you will spend most of your time putting out fires and keeping everyone happy)
9 Accept that at an event you are running, the host works the most and your opportunity to play will have to take a backseat to managing the event
10. Collapse in a heap at the end

I had become friends with many of the main people in the scene: the club owners, the suppliers, the people that were truly the movers and shakers of Toronto's kink. I loved a good party, and on off nights with no fetish events, I would invite them all to my house.

Soon we could no longer hold house parties because my neighbors would complain about all the spanking, cries of pain/pleasure and half-naked people coming in and out of the house. We moved up to venues around Toronto, renting local dungeon spaces for parties or friends' studio lofts. All the while I collected

Facing Page: Don't be afraid to take the leading role.

Silence is golden but duct tape is silver.

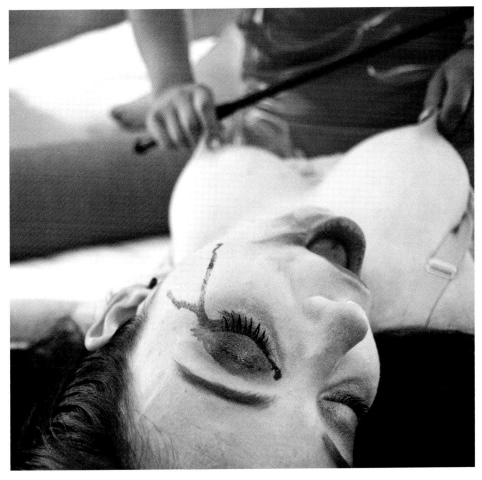

Squeeze your slaves nipples hard enough and they will cry delicious tears for you.

email addresses from friends so I could let everyone know where and when the next event would be. A random date at some random place, RanDOM Fetish Events took off. The warehouse parties would have three-hundred-plus people and the spaces I could find to rent just didn't have everything I needed to complete my vision.

The first party at the famous Reverb Night Club drew over five hundred people, selling out the venue, which featured local and international acts doing amazing stage performances. We decided to name this monthly party Sub-Space. Things have grown and grown and now in addition to SubSpace we also hold the yearly Torture Garden Toronto Weekend featuring four days and nights of fetish parties and workshop seminars.

—Craiger, SubSpace Fetish Night organizer, Toronto

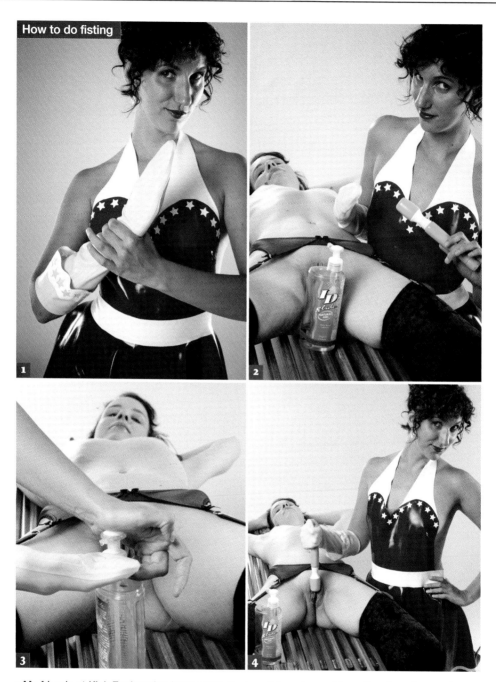

How to do fisting

1 My friends at Kink Engineering have created a long latex glove with no thumb or fingers, just for fisting. 2 Have your slave lay back on something comfortable and relax. There is no need to rush. 3 Use tons of lube. When in doubt, use more. Get the glove or your hand all wet and sloppy. 4 You can even warm them up with their favorite vibrator. Get them purring and their pussy or ass will relax to be more receptive to your hand.

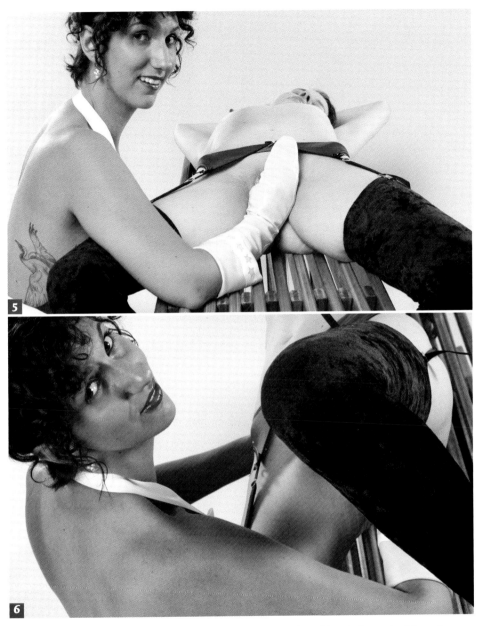

5 This glove makes it super easy to assume the proper hand position, but you don't have to have one. Take your fingers and fold all of them together to form a point. Tuck the thumb as you get closer to inserting it. **6** Take your time with the romance during fisting; slowly work your fingers in. When first penetrating, I always let the slave tell me when they are ready for more or for when they need me to hold still so they can relax until their body can get used to this new sensation. You can't rush into this, if you don't have the time to devote to a great session then find something else to do and come back to it.

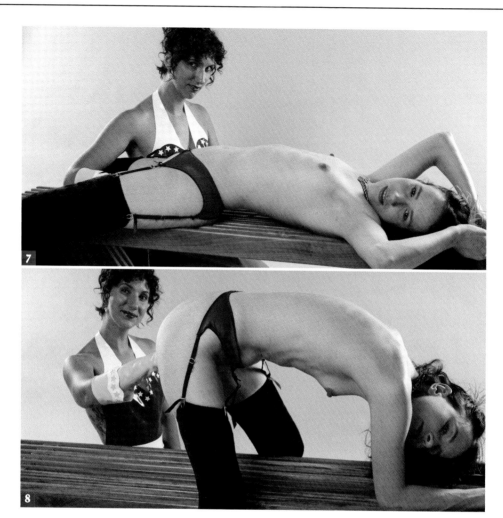

7 Slide it in more and more, gently twisting side to side. Think of yourself as "easing" into them rather than "pushing". The look on your slave's face should be like our lovely model here. If it isn't or is twisted and pained, you are going WAY too fast. This should be a sensual experience. Let them help guide you to the speed and depth. I have wide hands so getting past the saddle of my thumb is difficult so I never get past that and that is fine for me and my partners. For women or people with smaller hands you should be able to slip all the way in. Once you are in, please resist the urge to do any Muppet voices, no matter how tempting! **8** If you are doing it right and they are comfortable and relaxed, you can have them change positions gently. Face down and ass up is a powerfully submissive position. Some slaves love it when you do the in and out movement, some like the gentle twisting movement and still some just want you to be still so they can clench their internal muscles around you. For the Dominant it will feel like the tightest glove you have ever worn and if you remain still you may be able to feel their heartbeat. THAT is intimate.

9 Slow and steady and if you take your time there won't be any chance of tearing. Same with asses—go slow and work up to it. It isn't a race, its a sensual moment between two people.
10 If you are adventurous and experienced you can invite your friend for Double Penetration Fisting!

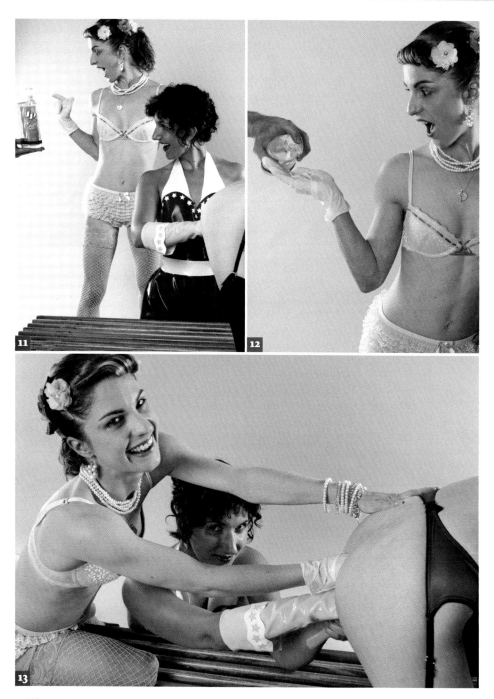

11 Why thank you Mr. Hand Model, I do believe the girls could use some more lube! 12 Use lots of lube; don't be shy! 13 If you are an experienced bottom with fisting and you can take it, having a hand in your vagina is sensual but having another one in your ass at the same time is exquisitely off the chart!

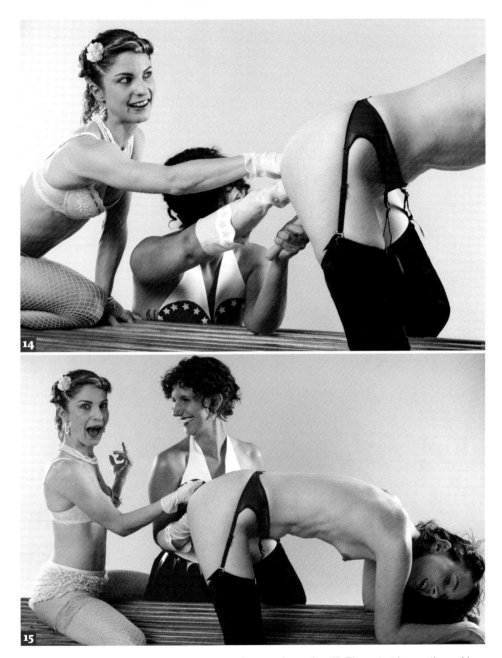

14 Have the person who is in the vagina stay there and remain still. Then start by gently working your fingers into the slave's bum. You HAVE to go slow; there isn't a lot of room in there. **15** As you work your way up and inside their ass, the slave may find they have to shift their position to accommodate "what all is going on back there". They may need to lift up their chest and for people who can experience orgasms from fisting this will be nirvana for them. Let them pick the best position for their enjoyment.

269

There is enough room for all in the scene—there is no reason to compete directly and attempt to steal others' participants. Think about what you want to offer—a munch, a monthly play party, a rave, a fun private party—and don't step on established toes. Take a look at the kink schedule for your city and arrange your event so that it does not directly compete with another. Then consider your target audience and the theme. Some organizers may want to put together an invite-only party for twenty of their closest friends and others might want to throw a two hundred–two thousand person bash. If you build it, they will come; it's all about giving back to the community and nurturing it. My own experience as an event organizer is as widely varied as my interests in kinky sex. I have run large pony play parties on private farms; organized and run workshops for international presenters, have organized munches and assisted others in running their own events, and performed at more than I can remember.

If you don't want to be the leader, you can help by volunteering your time and sweat. Everyone remembers help, such as picking up and delivering equipment, organizing food and water or even helping at the door. If you are an event organizer or aspire to be, initially volunteer your time at other fetish nights and let the organizers know you are thinking of offering up an alternative to what is currently on offer in your city. Be sincere about your help, ask them questions and make sure you are not just there to promote your event and scoop their audience. That is called "skating on someone else's event" and is very much frowned upon. Being respectful and helpful and spending time in your community before you try to organize an event will help build your reputation and show the established people that you are there to complement, not complicate, the events that already exist. When you have decided you are going to be the leader and are putting it all together for the first time, remember that the delegation of duties is important but no one should ever delegate something they are not willing to do themselves. Lead from the front and by example. You should be willing to schlep equipment from venue to venue, stack cases of water, or figure out where the DJ should set up, and not just ask someone else to do it. Still, we can't do it all, and this is particularly important lesson to learn if you are a Dominant. We like to think we can do it all, and that

As well as the ends from balloons, o-rings for piercings can make great nipple rings.

Facing Page: Sensory deprivation can be as simple as a blindfold and earphones.

Pigtails make
excellent handles.

everything relies on us. But there are people who want to help, and it is important to tap those resources available to you. A bit of advice that has always shaped my events over the years was given to me years ago by my mentor: "After a party, a good leader has people saying, 'Boy he put on a great party!' and a GREAT leader has people saying, 'Boy WE put on a great party!' afterward." Let people feel they are a part of something larger than themselves, lead by example, and you will find that you have many people willing to help. Some of the benefits of organizing your own event are:

- You get to throw the party you want
- You get to invite the people you want
- You get to create an environment that is positive and welcoming
- You can have a lot of fun!

Of course there are some downsides to organizing an event yourself, and the largest one is, again, "the host works the most." You will be so busy setting up the event and helping organize things and keeping the flow going that you most likely will not even have a chance to play that night. I volunteer or just attend someone else's party for the fun times, and when I have my own event I know I will be working my ass off and won't usually have much time for play, if at all. Helping at others' parties keeps you active and engaged with the other people organizing events in your city. A little face time with other organizers and some appropriate compliments will go a long way. We are all in this together; we should all want to help each other, otherwise the scene will eat itself due to competition and that is never pretty and leads to a fragmented community.

Bound for Glory

As an organizer of events, you will find that eventually the media will come knocking on your door when they need a sound bite—a small quote that will frame a piece on kinky sex they are working on. Your local and national media outlets are forever curious about our scene and some will want to present it in a sensational light, while others may want to present it with sincerity. My biggest question when I am approached to give a quote or sound bite is, "How is this going to be used and what is your intent as a broadcaster?" I only give sound bites or assistance to TV shows like "Sex Matters" if they demonstrate that they are going to present our scene in a positive light and not make it into an episode of Jerry Springer. They will

How to remove latex clothing

1 Slipping out of your latex after a hard night of partying is easy in the shower. **2** Get all wet and use a mild soap. **3** Soap yourself alllllllll over, you want the soap to run under the latex.

273

4 It will slip right down your arms... 5 and off. 6 Then wriggle it down over your hips.

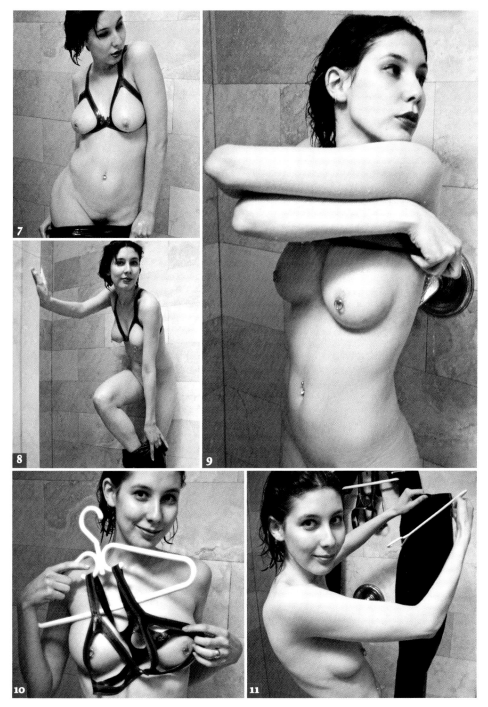

7 Oooh yeah, keep on wriggling! 8 Let the soap and water slip it off, there is no need to tug.

9 Then pull the rest up and over your head. 10 Hang each piece on a separate hanger.

11 Only use plastic hangers, not wood or metal.

The life of a fetish model is a lot of things, but it is never dull.

need you to sign a release form, typically ahead of time before the interview or just after, and always before they edit it. If you suspect they are going to reframe your words in a light that is not positive, then you should refuse to sign away the rights for it or better yet decline the interview. Be careful what you are signing. Once you are on camera and have signed the release form they can do whatever they want with it and it is theirs forever. Choose your words carefully; the scene needs positive exposure, not a "Gong Show." It can be a reciprocal relationship. My recent experience with a documentary film crew making *Comfortable? I Can Fix That...*, a film on the rope bondage scene in Toronto, led the producer and director and myself through meeting after meeting as I outlined my concerns about the presentation of the final product. What would his angle be? How were they planning on editing it all together, and who would the final audience be? After alleviating all my concerns and demonstrating their sincerity in presenting the rope bondage scene in a positive light, I went ahead and cooperated and they shot it and I was able to introduce the production people to many, many more people in the scene that were perfect for the documentary than they would have been able to meet, being outsiders. The film is now shown at short documentary film festivals around the world. We got exposure in a positive way and they got access to the scene because they were respectful and sincere—a win-win situation for both of us!

Crying is not a safe word.

Smile…

Speaking of cameras, as an organizer you are always going to need to set a camera policy for your event. This can be addressed by having a sign and policy that says, NO CAMERAS TONIGHT, PLEASE or CAMERAS ARE ALL RIGHT IF THE SHOT DOESN'T INCLUDE ANYONE OTHER THAN YOUR PARTNER at events, or distributing different-colored wristbands to the attendees. People who wear the blue wristbands are camera shy, while the ones wearing yellow are camera sluts and are happy to be photographed. By having this policy explained in a smiling, courteous and respectful manner at the door, we are **ALL** made responsible; it gives reassurance to others who will be attending who'll be happy to alert the PM or organizer if they see someone breaching the policy. Lots of us don't want to be photographed and the rest of us are going to respect those boundaries. Most of us are probably more open about photos while we are playing at home, knowing that we have control of the pictures.

The day after a harsh spanking will give your slave the chance to relive the scene every time they sit down.

Some people love being exhibitionists for the camera: it turns them on and excites them. For those people, with time and the flexibility to travel, there is a way to make a living at being a fetish model in the professional world of the fetish adult market.

Nurse, Flight Attendant…Fetish Model?

This is a career that is *not* in the high school career development curriculum! It involves a living out of a suitcase, traveling to new cities every week, shooting new and interesting content and having to navigate between the slippery worlds of producers who are established and well known and some guy with a camera who wants to film you putting on opera-length gloves for an hour. It can be exciting and unique but also exhausting, with all the travel. The rewards are great—travel, meeting and working with interesting people and making good money doing something you probably would have done for free just because you are interested in kink to begin with.

My career as a fetish model began somewhat by coincidence. I wanted to know if I could do it and more importantly, what it would be like? Five years later, I have discovered that I enjoy fetish modeling—the feeling of ropes on my skin, the delight of restraint and powerlessness, the surge of pain coupled with the pleasure that comes immediately afterward. The sensations are intense and raw and each shoot has taught me something about myself. I have learned not only what I like but what I can handle. BDSM has often been criticized by feminists and others who feel that a disempowered woman is a complicated notion. For me, engaging in BDSM has been contrary to those critiques. When I am shooting or playing, I feel completely empowered to give over control and instead focus on my own sexual pleasure and chaotic mind. When my sexual power is in the hands of someone else, I find I am alone with myself and my sensations. I can relax into the enjoyment of the moment and what I am feeling. I may not be able to move, may only be able to grunt or drool, but I am more able than ever to touch my pleasure, to get inside the pain and become galvanized by going through it and seeing how strong I am. I have always felt very strongly that a woman should be able to determine what is hot for her.
—Dylan Ryan, fetish actress

Facing Page: Your slave can come in handy in many ways!

Adding a little hair bondage will always make kinky sex more interesting.

Becoming a fetish model is a consuming process that requires timing, an open mind, discipline, and the ability to think outside the box. There is nothing conventional about the career of a fetish model. One day you might find yourself tied snuggly in a rope bondage harness and another day you might find yourself rubbing balloons over yourself while you are dressed as a kitty cat. The work is diverse and unique; after all, it caters to the wide gamut of fetishes. If you feel you simply cannot take on a photo shoot job where you will have your shoes licked by an actor lying on the floor wrapped like a burrito in a shower curtain, then this is not the job for you. There is nothing conventional about the shoots you will do, but therein lies their strength. Because the work is unique and no day is the same as the last, you will constantly be stimulated and engaged. There is a constant debate as to whether or not you should be allowed to bring an escort to a shoot. My own guidelines for a shoot are that a model can bring an escort if that person is going to remain in the background and be unobtrusive. There is nothing

A good fetish model needs to be in shape both physically and mentally.

Pop rocks are a
fun addition to
any blowjob!

worse than a grumpy boyfriend standing in the background and constantly challenging a shoot or trying to direct his girlfriend who is trying to get her fetish modeling career started. I won't work under those circumstances. Keep in mind I have worked to maintain a reputation for being a fun, respectful photographer and one that models feel safe around. It is a reputation I have built one model at a time and I cherish the trust they put in me. Keep this in mind during your own career trajectory. Not all of my models bring escorts; ones I have worked with for a long time or those that I know very well usually show up for a shoot with all their suitcases jam packed with outfits and equipment and with no escort in sight. I find, for myself as a photographer , if I welcome the escorts for the first several sessions, it becomes easier to manage their presence as the work and sessions evolve. Conversely, if you are a model going to your first shoot and the photographer says, "No escorts"—trust the feeling in your tummy. If it doesn't add up, then politely and respectfully decline the offer to shoot. You don't have to be bitchy and rude. A simple "I understand where you are coming from, but at this point, just starting out, I would feel more comfortable bringing my escort. Perhaps in the future we can work together but for now, I think we should postpone this," does a few things for you. It

■ Establishes your boundaries of needing an escort

■ Shows you are polite and respectful and above all else, professional

■ Demonstrates you are not closed to working together in the future, just not right now

Getting Started

The first thing you are going to need to do is to build your portfolio. This is a time in a model's career that will bring you into contact with unknown photographers and other models. It is also a time of low pay, if you're paid at all—the "TFP" time of your career. TFP stands for "Trade for Pics." As you build your portfolio, you will be asked by photographers, especially new ones, to enter into this symbiotic relationship with them where you shoot for free with them in exchange for the images you will mutually share. It is where all of us in the industry start. This can be a time of immense growth and some incredibly creative work, when you are both exploring

Facing Page: RAWR! Kitty wants to play!

A julienned slice of ginger can be slid down the urethra for an eye opening experience. Leave a bulb on the end so it doesn't disappear.

the possibilities of fetish photography and video work. My own career as a fetish photographer began with me shooting my friends. I would ask them to come get all dressed up and we would spend an afternoon or evening shooting outside on location: behind Dumpsters, near industrial lofts, in dingy alleyways and abandoned buildings or even in soybean fields. The images I created back then were raw, edgy and interesting in their somewhat primitive technical way. I started shooting with a 1.3 megapixel camera. That was cutting edge in the handheld, point-and-shoot camera world circa 2001. I would take my camera along on hikes through forests with my models, exploring composition and lighting and figuring out the logistics of trying to tie up a model and photograph her all at the same time. It was hard work doing all the rope bondage *and* shooting at the same time, but there was something magical about those days— I was unencumbered, traveling fast and light. My images were good; I had been to art school and had a strong fundamental foundation in composition and lighting. But this isn't to say you need to go to art school before you start shooting—in fact you should just start shooting and doing your own research. My initial work brought me notice from the various professional dungeons around the city when they needed to have promotional pictures of their employees and facilities shot. This in turn led to me meeting more people who were filming fetish video work and my business and exposure increasing until I was having art gallery shows and getting a few books under my belt. Being a fetish photographer is its own book; here we're concentrating more on the modeling side of the equation. But I can't mention one without at least touching on the other. If you are a beginning photographer, you have to understand that the models exist to work professionally with us. Be respectful and courteous. Make sure the intent and focus of the shoot is explained in detail before you both agree to shoot and whether or not there is to be any compensation—cash or TFP. Your reputation as a photographer is dependant on the models. If you are known as someone who is just in the industry to get laid, then word will travel fast and no one will shoot with you. There should be no surprises about the subject matter at the shoot. If you want to be a respected photographer, it pays to discuss the content of the shoot before the day arrives when you are to work together. Don't let the model show up and spring, "Oh, by the way, after we do the pinup stuff, I was thinking that we could do some really intimate things to you with this basket of garden vegetables while

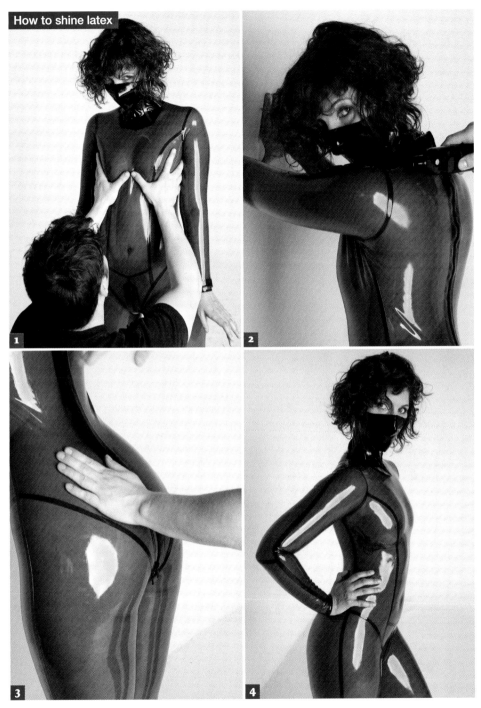

How to shine latex

1 When you shine up a latex outfit, you can use the super expensive latex shine they sell...

2 or you can use a silicone based lube. 3 The main thing is you get to rub them alllllll over while

putting it on! 4 All shined up and ready for action!

Yes you can go swimming in your latex and look fabulous doing it!

you're wearing rubber boots." That is really uncool. Your work shouldn't be surprising to them. There *are* parts of a shoot that will go in a different direction as you both get inspiration during it; that is part of the creative process. But you should both have a general outline of what is going to happen and what the agreed upon boundaries are. On the other hand, if you are respectful, fun and professional to work with, you will have many doors open to you as models tell other models about how great you are to work with.

If you're going to pursue a modeling career, you have to take care of yourself: eat right, work out, do yoga, get a good night's sleep. This is all advice you would expect to get from your mom, right? But it plays a key role in your longevity as a fetish model. This type of work can be physically demanding and mentally taxing, coupled with being a nomad, living out of your suitcase and coordinating travel. It's also true that fetish porn conventions like FetishCon are a hell of a lot of fun. The parties are truly legendary. And it is important to blow off steam once in a while; have fun and party, but make it the exception, not the rule. I have seen some wonderful models over the years wind up getting washed out of the bottom of the industry because they started the partying lifestyle and just kept up long after they should have taken a break and taken care of themselves. One of my favorite models in the industry, Wenona, is extremely professional, does yoga daily, works out, watches her diet, is well read and goes to conventions to work, and is in bed by 11:00 p.m. Doesn't sound like a sexy lifestyle does it? But she has been doing it for eight years and takes such good care of herself that she expects do to it for at least another ten. That is a professional attitude that producers and directors will respect and like working with.

Lets take a look at what you do once you have enough images stocked away; how do you get exposure? Thankfully the Internet can assist in a big way. There are great sites online that are devoted to helping models find work, such as modelmayhem.com—both vanilla modeling and fetish and kink and other adult modeling. You can also find a community of photographers on social networking sites such as fetlife.com and, to a certain extent, on vanilla social networking sites. Be forewarned, though, some of the more vanilla social networking sites are quite draconian about removing any adult-related material that you might be used to in the fetish modeling world. A close friend of mine, Maxine X, continually has to recreate

Having a removable cracker on your single tail whip will ensure that you use a new cracker for each new partner and that will limit cross contamination.

287

her profiles on those vanilla sites since her profile and images keep getting deleted by the admin. It is like a cat and mouse game for her business. However, in terms of exposure, these three sites will get you an audience that is much larger than what would traditionally be accomplished the old-school way. Once you get your images, creating a profile is as easy as posting your pictures online. Consistency is important once you create a profile; keep the content in several profiles similar so that if someone is looking for the next big thing, *i.e.*, you, they have more than one chance of finding and contacting you. Nothing is more frustrating for a photographer or production company than to have glimpsed someone who would be perfect for a shoot and then not be able to find them again.

Your Own Webpage

I also recommend that once you get response from the social networking sites, you create a webpage for yourself. It doesn't have to be super slick and fancy. Let the porn companies worry about those issues with their own content—banners and pop-ups and the like. There are so many templates available and domain and hosting fees are so incredibly low, there's no reason not to do it. Your site should be easy to navigate and demonstrate a wide variety of poses and the looks you are capable of. What it shouldn't contain is annoying music, pop-ups or a url that isn't simple to understand and remember. You want production companies to be able to remember your name and contact you easily, so come up with something that will stay at the forefront of their mind and they can easily remember. A long time ago I knew a pro domme who had a great little business and was doing very well. Then out of the blue she decided that a name change would be just the right thing for her. For some reason she decided to pick a symbol as her new name, a symbol that didn't have an easily pronounced word version—sort of like when Prince changed his name to a symbol and everyone had to refer to him as The Artist Formerly Known As Prince. She changed her webpage and her content and her advertising to this new symbol and when people did call her for work, they didn't even know how to address her since her new name was a symbol. What do you think happened to her business? Yep, it dried up and she is long gone…and mostly forgotten.

Keep your url easy to remember. RubberChick.com is much easier to remember than bitchgoddessvanessadesimone.com.

Both model and photographer should feel satisfied with and proud of the work they've done.

Safe and Bound

A key issue for any model, established or just starting out in the industry, is safety. There will be times when you will be bound and gagged and unable to speak in a clear way. You need to know the parameters and expectations of the shoot and what your employers are willing to do to ensure that you are safe. How knowledgeable are they? How safe are they? Finding other models that have worked with them is key. Ask them for references or find out if they have a website on which you can see their content. Ask them blunt questions; there should be no surprises about what is going to happen once the shoot gets underway. If you are not expecting to be penetrated and it suddenly comes up that "this is what we are doing next," and you are bound and gagged, you will be in a much more difficult position to get out of than if you had previously negotiated. You should also be forthcoming about any health issues that could come up as a result of the shoot: Old torn rotator cuff? Asthma? The producer needs to know your limitations and concerns so that he or she can produce hot and sexy content form which you both walk away happy. You are going to trust this person to keep you safe through the shoot and trust is a two-way street. You will have your limits pushed and boundaries tested; this is part of what attracts us to this work. You have to be able to be tested in a good way without having a mental collapse. Limits can be sexual, or regarding pain or bondage. You might enjoy hardcore flogging and whipping but once you get tied up, you get claustrophobic. Ideally, shoots can be super fun and enjoyable! Everyone's limits are different and you need to know yours and where your line is. If a producer wants you to push way past your boundaries and you are not comfortable with that, don't do it. It is easier to recover if you go slow when you are starting out, than if you go too far too fast. What matters most at the end of the day is that when the shoot is finished, you not only feel good about the work you have done but you are proud of yourself for what you accomplished.

Doggie style makes it easy to change holes depending on your mood!

Afterward

You had a great shoot and you are still feeling the endorphins. What do you want to do to decompress? Go running? Spend time with a friend? Get your

Facing Page: Imagine the look on your grandchildren's faces when you show them what Nanny used to do for a living!

There is nothing more beautiful than a vulnerable bottom clad in rope.

magic wand out and masturbate like a banshee? You need to take time afterward to discharge the energy you built up over the shoot. You can pamper yourself: spending time in a bath of epsom salts will do wonders at soothing aching muscles. If you have done a lot of percussion play, you would do well to apply Traumeel (a topical ointment) that will reduce bruising. When juggling shoots, you have to keep your schedule in mind when agreeing to certain activities. Can you schedule a caning video for the end of the week, while you do the bondage footage in the beginning? That way you won't have bruising through the other work and can take a few days to heal before starting your next week's work. Production companies will be sensitive to this request if you explain how your schedule is shaping up. No one wants you to come to a sexy silk stocking video shoot if your butt looks like hamburger because of the bullwhip work you did the day before. You must take care of yourself so that you can continue to do this work on a long-term basis without burning out and compromising your boundaries.

Being a pro comes with its challenges but also has a lot of rewards, and whether you're organizing big events, working as a fetish photographer or building a career as a fetish model, you are going to be faced with unique and interesting challenges that will require you to be open, honest and respectful to your colleagues and other professionals in the industry. At times it will feel like you are juggling too many balls in the air but starting out on a manageable level and growing at a pace that you are comfortable with will reap you great rewards and help your longevity in the adult fetish world. The challenges can deflate you at times but remember, the only sled dog with a decent view is the one in the front.

> Aftercare is even more important following humiliation play than a straight up beating, because of the emotional overload involved.

Five Key Points for Longevity as a Pro in the Kinky World:

■ Create a fetish event where the theme complements rather than competes with other events

■ Be respectful of people who don't want to be photographed

■ Own your own URL, don't let someone else buy it and develop it for you

■ As a model, take care of yourself physically and emotionally: know what you need to do after a shoot to regain your personal balance

■ As a photographer, respect the models and discuss what you want to shoot long before you actually get them in front of the camera

Chapter Ten

And Finally...

After the game, the king and the pawn go into the same box
— *Italian Proverb*

I have noticed, in the kinky lifestyle, that just when I think I have seen it all, along comes something new. Innovation is always leading the way in BDSM; people into kinky sex are super-creative motherfuckers; some of the creativity I have seen over the years merits an engineering award. Sometimes I wonder if *being* in the scene makes you more creative, or if the more creative types of personalities are just naturally drawn to the scene. There is definitely a level of innovation in kinky sex that is lacking elsewhere in interpersonal relationships.

My hope is that in this book I will have introduced readers to some topics that have never been covered in other publications. Certain of these activities can be very edgy and risky, but making knowledge available is the best way to ensure that people have a good chance of playing without getting hurt or hurting someone else. Educating yourself about these activities and situations also means taking responsibility for engaging in them. Only you can protect yourself. A lot of what we do is risky. People have been indulging in kinky erotic play from time immemorial; there is nothing new about spanking or whipping other individuals or tying them up and having your way with them. HOW you do it makes it your own. There is nothing new under the sun except for how you do it.

The higher the risk, the hotter kinky play is for some people. After all people skydive and rock climb and go shoe shopping at the mall during Christmas because they love a good rush. Other people get the same thrill through kinky sex. You know that point where time stretches out infinitely, when the noise of the outside world falls away and your entire world becomes just you and your partner? You could be in a crowded dungeon or pushing your lover

Facing Page: Inspect and appraise your slave daily.

It's very easy to fall in love with a beautifully made flogger.

up against the wall in a back alley barely out of sight of the passing pedestrians, kissing her and twisting her nipples, while her high heels scrape across the pavement as she tries to keep her ragged moan of desire half buried in her throat. It is in such moments of sexual abandonment that I hope having read this book will help you to do whatever you want to do, more safely. We want to play over and over again with trust *building*, not crumbling, and the only way you can do that is by openly communicating with your partner and building upon your knowledge and personal education. Some people say that higher risk leads to more reckless activities. I disagree. I believe that with compassion and empathy, we can explore harder edge play with eyes wide open and an understanding and acceptance of responsibility that comes with it. As sexual renegades we are constantly pushing the boundaries of ourselves and our partners, at the same time seeking a greater understanding of who we are and how we fit into our world.

Care, compassion and respect: three simple words, easy to remember,

Facing Page: Star Trek would have been much more interesting if they'd used dildo guns.

How to Be Kinkier

With a few toys and a dirty mind, you can find yourself anywhere with a kinky lifestyle.

When making and using an ice dildo, make sure you double up the condom on it or else you will have one very unhappy submissive and one hell of a "fishing trip" story on your hands.

but in the ego-gratifying world of kinky sex, quickly forgotten in the heat of the moment. That is what gives trust its value—that it determinedly rides along a hurricane of desire. I have always advised that when presented with something you aren't interested in but that your partner really wants, be open minded and give it a chance, as long as you don't compromise your own safety or security. There are times when you can make concessions and times when you need to stand firm. You might discover something you never knew you liked until you tried it!

Compassion is what sets us apart from the psychotic; also empathy and care. We all run into people in the scene who are in it for all the wrong reasons and they typically crash and burn, but not before hurting a few genuine people who are good for the community. It is essential that we in the kinky community communicate openly so that this behavior isn't accepted. The key people to learn from are those who have years in the scene; the ones who have stood the test of time and continued to put together munches, workshops, conferences and fetish nights; the ones who work tirelessly to make sure that YOU have the best chance to enjoy yourself safely and happily in the community. Ask about them; their reputations

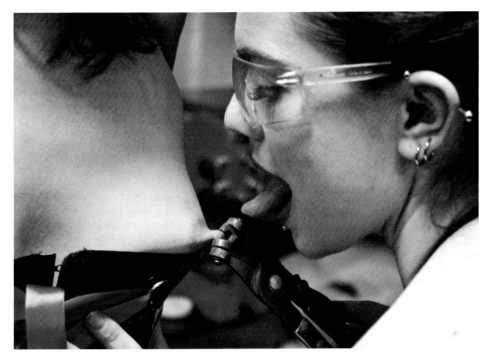

Improvised nipple clamps can be made out of almost anything as long as you have a creative mind.

should precede them. After all, once you strip away all the leather and latex and kinky restraints and other masks of the fantastic, whether you are in a 24/7 M/s relationship or just like to explore on the weekends, all we have left is our character and reputation. Guard yours and strengthen it and surround yourself with others who do the same.

The joy of raw sexuality is that the participants are stripped down to their primal essence with no pretense and no masking of who they are. You can leave behind your work world, your soccer mom or fixer role. This is one of the last bastions of personal freedom in our society, where we can truly let go and vulnerably expose our desires in the sexual realm and revel in that. Above everything else, let's not forget the joy that we experience. Some speak of the spiritual journey that kinky sex can take them on; others seek transcendence through whips, floggers and technical expertise, but most important is the joy of exploration with a partner you care about. Without that sense of joy in the exploration of body and soul and connection with your partner, kinky play can never be as fulfilling. Your sexuality is one of the most precious things you have; make positive choices about whom you share and explore it with.

Resources

Works Cited

- *How to Be Kinky: A Beginner's Guide to BDSM* Morpheous, Green Candy Press, San Francisco CA 2008
- *A Guide to Sexual Misery* Bernhard Ludwig Uberreuter, Wien 2005
- *Bound to be free* Chales Moster and JJ Madeson Continuum NY 2000
- *On The Safe Edge: A Manual for SM Play* Trevor Jacques WholeSM Publishing Toronto 1993

Suggested Reading

- *Two Knotty Boys Showing You the Ropes*, Two Knotty Boys, Green Candy Press, San Francisco CA 2006
- *Two Knotty Boys Back On The Ropes*, Two Knotty Boys, Green Candy Press, San Francisco CA 2010
- *SM 101* Jay Wiseman, Greenery Press San Francisco 1998
- *Erotic Bondage Handbook*, Jay Wiseman Greenery Press San Francisco, 2000
- *The Master's Manual: A Handbook of Erotic Dominance*, Jack Rinella, Daedalus Publishing Company, 1994
- *Erotic Surrender: The Sensual Joys of Female Submission*, Claudia Varrin, Citadel 2003
- *Miss Abernathy's Concise Slave Training Manual* Christine Abernathy, Greenery Press 1998
- *The Bride Wore Black Leather...And He Looked Fabulous!: An Etiquette Guide for the Rest of Us* Drew Campbell Greenery Press 2000

Toy makers and artisans

This is by no means a comprehensive list, during my travels I meet many wonderful toy makers and artisans of kinky toys and speaking from personal experience these are some of my most favorites. The great thing

Facing Page: Who wouldn't want to know more?

301

is that I am always discovering new everywhere I go. There are lots of online resources run by individuals in your local area. Google is your best friend. Support your local artisans so they can support you!

Rope

I exclusively use these rope makers for all of my teaching and personal use:

Handmade Rope	handmaderope.com
Serenity Bound	serenity-bound.com

Other great rope makers and suppliers

Madam Butterfly	butterflyrope.com
Maui Kink	mauikink.com
Aja Rope	ajarope.com
Shibari Ropes	shibariropes.com
Twisted Monk	twistedmonk.com
Kinky Ropes	kinkyropes.com
Beautiful Bondage UK	beautifulbondage.net

Clothing and Toys

Northbound Leather	northboundleather.com
Come As You Are	comeasyouare.com
Latex Vac Beds	kinkengineering.com
Ego Assassin Latex Designs	ego-assassin.com
Master Andre	masterandre.com
Aslan Leather	aslanleather.com
Toy Cases	foryournymphomation.com
Steampunk Vibrators	littledeathray.com
Fetish jewelry	fetjeweller.com
Bellakoi Designs	bellakoidesigns.com
Alice Handle	alicehandle.com
Torvea	torvea.com
Priape	priape.com
Hot Wax	mild-to-wild.com
Floggers	kaosfloggers.com
Rosie's Floggers	rosiesfloggers.com
Venus Envy (Halifax and Ottawa)	venusenvy.ca
Ponce	jewelrybyponceportland.com

Atelier Gothique	ateliergothique.com
Axovus	axovus.com
Nipple Charms	nipplecharms.com
Girdles	girdlebound.com
Heartwood Whips	heartwoodwhips.com
Mailler Phong Chainmail	cgmaille.com
Leather toys	katanaworks.com
Corsets	fittobetied.ca
Ms. Martha's Corsets	corset1.com
Whips	whipmaker.ca
	masterwhipmaker.com
	snakewhips.com
Libido toys	libidolondon.com
The Wild Side Cross Dressing	wildside.org
The Stockroom	stockroom.com
Mr. S. Leather	mr-s-leather.com
Extreme Restraints	extremerestraints.com
Burlesque supplies	bettiesandbombshells.com
Bear T shirts	beartshirts.com
Canes	canes4pain.com
	thekinkshop.com
Leather Masks and canes	prysmcreations.com
CheapTRX	cheaptrx.com
Master of Toys	motbdsm.com
Aluminum handled floggers	floggers.com
Restraints	luckystarsleather.com
Floggers	kinkykustoms.ca
	flogger.com
Rings	triskeliondesigns.com
Sensuous Bliss	etsy.com/shop/sensuousbliss
Chastity Devices	lockedinsteel.com
	wholesalebdsm.com
Fort Troff	forttroff.com
Kinky Medical	kinkymedical.com
Venus Eromedia	venuseromedia.be
Rubber Fucker Latex	rubberfucker.com
Paddles	spankinc.ca

Steel toys	bluediamondtradingco.com
Violet Wand	violetwandstore.com
Healsfang	healsfang.com
Fantasies in Leather	fantasiesinleather.com
Dr. Clockwork	drclockwork.com
Fire play and medical toys	mtslenterprises.com
Good Vibrations	goodvibes.com
Coco De Mer	cocodemerusa.com
Babeland	babeland.com
Self Serve	selfservetoys.com
Australia: Leather Gear	eagleleather.com.au
Ireland: BDSM toys	toysforjoys.ie

BDSM B&B and other kinky accomodations

Ontario	chateausauble.ca
	warmbuns.ca
Seattle	mybdsm.com/pages/GypsyArms/
	seascene.htm
Oregon	twistedcedarestate.com
Amsterdam	absolutesuite.com
UK	essandemm.com
France	frenchdungeon.com
Spain	sm-urlaub-mallorca.com
Italy	casacarisma.it
Jamaica	kinkinthecaribbean.com
New Zealand	bdsmpassion.com
Australia	dragonhousefarm.com.au

Magazines online and paper

Eros	eros-zine.com
Domination Directory International	ddimag.com
Skin Two	skintwo.co.uk
Marquis	marquis.de
Secret	secretmag.com

Bookstores and kinky cafés

Come As You Are (Toronto)	comeasyouare.com

St. Louis	shamelessgrounds.com
Outwrite Books (Atlanta)	outwritebooks.com
A Different Light (San Francisco)	adlbooks.com

Websites of hot online sites and art

Mine	lordmorpheous.com
	modelmayhem.com/812653
Maxine X	maxinex.com
Candle Boxxx	candleboxxx.com
Chloe Bond	chloebond.com
Artemis Hunter	artemishunter.com
Kink.com	kink.com
Chanta Rose	chantasbitches.com
JB Roper	jbroper.com
The Beautiful Kind	thebeautifulkind.com
Lew Rubens	boundndetermined.com

Educational/ Conferences and Advocacy groups

Canada

Northbound (Toronto)	northboundlive.com
Torture Garden Toronto (Toronto)	torturegardentoronto.com
Toronto TNG	torontotng.com
Black and Blue Ball (Winnepeg)	blackandblueball.ca
Breathless (Ottawa)	breathlessottawa.com
Montreal Fetish Weekend (Montreal)	fetishweekend.com
Northern Exposure (Sudbury)	snobears.ca
EHBC (Southern Ontario)	ehbc.ca
Vancouver Dungeon (with car pooling!)	vancouverdungeon.com
Lupercalia (Edmonton)	lupercalia-edmonton.com
Libido (Vancouver)	libidoevents.com
519 LGBT community centre (Toronto)	the519.org

U.S.

National Coalition of Sexual Freedom (San Francisco)	ncsfreedom.org

LA KinkBall Fetish Weekend (LA, CA)	lakinkball.com
Southplains Leather Fest (Dallas)	southplainsleatherfest.com
Thunder in the Mountains (Colorado)	thunderinthemountains.com
Pony Play(Russell Springs)	dulca-scenes.org
The Floating World (New Jersey)	floatingworld.dreamhosters.com
TES (NYC)	tes.org
Miss Rubber World (NYC)	nyrubberball.com
IML (Chicago)	imrl.com
Beyond Leather (Fort Lauderdale)	beyondleather.net
Black Rose (Maryland)	br.org
N.O.B.L.E. (New Orleans)	lanoble.org
Shibaricon (Chicago)	shibaricon.com
Knot Guilty (Atlanta)	knotguilty.org
DomCon (Atlanta)	domconatlanta.com
Atlanta Bound (Atlanta)	atlantabound.com
St.Louis	STL3.com
Lewbaricon (travelling)	lewbaricon.com
C.L.A.W. (Cleveland)	clawinfo.org
Mid Atlantic Leather (Washington)	leatherweekend.com
Colonial Kink (Williamsburg):	colonialkink.com
Northern Exposure (Anchorage)	ne2010.net

Europe and UK:

Boudoir Bizarre (Zaandam, Netherlands)	boudoir-bizarre.nl
Mr. Rubber Italy (Rome, Italy)	lcroma.com
Evolution Fetish (Stoke on Trent, UK)	atlantisevolution.co.uk/evolution_fetish.html

Carribean

Paradise Bound (Dominican Republic)	kinkevents.com/cff/pervypeople.html
Kink in the Carribean (Negril, Jamaica)	kinkinthecaribbean.com/kinkx/

Kinky Furniture makers

Porte Rouge   porterouge.net/pr/Home

Dating and Online BDSM sites:

Fetlife   fetlife.com

Bondage   bondage.com

Museums and Archives

Amsterdam Sex Museum: sexmuseumamsterdam.nl

NYC Sex Museum: museumofsex.com

Leather Archives and Museum   leatherarchives.org
 (Chicago)

Sex worker and other resources

Toronto

Maggies   maggiestoronto.ca

Sex Professionals of Canada   spoc.ca/index.html

A.C.T.   actoronto.org

Montreal

Stella   chezstella.org

San Francisco

Health Resources   bayswan.org

New York

Spread Magazine   spreadmagazine.org

Sex Workers Project   sexworkersproject.org/

Listings for therapists/counselors in Ontario:

■ Daniel Zimmerman, M.S.W., 7 - 348 Lacasse Ave., Ottawa, Ontario, K1L
7A9, 613-741-0606, Dsottawa@sympatico.ca

■ Fadi Abou-Rihan, Ph.D., 202 - 2 College Street, Toronto, 416-964-6357,
http://psychotherapytoronto.info/sexuality.html

■ Nick Mulé, Ph.D., RSW, Suite 820, 77 Maitland Place, Toronto, Ontario,
Canada M4Y 2V6, Phone: 416-926-9135. Individuals, couples, families.
Various BDSM issues.

■ Peggy J. Kleinplatz, Ph.D., C. Psych., C, 161 Frank St., Ottawa, Ontario, K2P 0X4, Canada, 613-563-0846, email: kleinpla@uottawa.ca. Sex therapy with individuals, couples and groups.

■ Terri Lyn Lemon, ABA Therapist, Michigan and Southern Ontario, based in Windsor, terrilynlemon@comcast.net Metro Detroit, Flint, Lansing, Windsor areas.

The Models

Models

Elle, Kittehlicious, Ava Destruction, Doll, Brittany, Babygap, Greg, SLam, Russian Bear, Little Rose, Annie, Bella Noir, Jon Henderson, WyldAura, Fire Domination, The Red Rocket, Tragedy Ann, Nadia Versace, Aeva, Mandy the Halfcast Moon, Amu, Tanya Rigley, Dylan Ryan, Lyarah, Rain Daniels and Vaeda.

And those with weblinks

Alec & Chloe Bond	chloebond.com
Archean	modelmayhem.com/1257597
Kerry Maguire	modelmayhem.com/596363
Nyssa Nevers	nyssasneverland.com
Katy Cee	modelmayhem.com/687335
Tina Timebalm	modelmayhem.com/285662
Bri Playter	modelmayhem.com/629431
Wenona	modelmayhem.com/25021
Nicotine	modelnicotine.com
Kyla Blair	modelmayhem.com/1816408
Melissa Dale-Hicks	modelmayhem.com/2008952
Kat Reznor	modelmayhem.com/1300712
Katrina Razor	modelmayhem.com/2105178
Siren Thorn	sirenthorn.com
Allyss	modelmayhem.com/1767040
Deanna Deadly	deannadeadly.com
Andriana Santos	andrianasantos.com
Amazon Syren	modelmayhem.com/1005204
Droidsy	modelmayhem.com/230678
Laura Unbound	lauraunbound.com
PXE	modelmayhem.com/505070

Goddess Shea	goddessshea.com/
Orabella	modelmayhem.com/627686
Melissa Masters	modelmayhem.com/856616
Mad Scientist	kinkengineering.com
Sybil Hawthorne	sybilhawthorne.com
Ego Assassin	ego-assassin.com
Kaze	modelmayhem.com/1496988
Jezabel Knight	jezabelknight.com
Sandy Gabriel	modelmayhem.com/572038

Studios and Media Support

Video production	bluemyst.com
Geoff George Photography	geoffgeorge.com
The Oh Team	theohteam.com
FAT CAT Photography	modelmayhem.com/902307
Creative Image Studios	creativeimagestudios.com
SubSpace Studio	subspacestudio.com
Sex Matters	cp24.com/sexmatters
Fat Cat Studio	modelmayhem.com/902307

Special Thanks to

Once again my editor, Kevin, who has helped polish my words again and who I'm surprised still puts up with nonsense. The Cundari Agency for pimping me out. All of the models that grace these pages for giving of their time selflessly and supporting this project during its development. You are all consummate professionals and I couldn't have done it without you. Elle and Effi for putting up with my shenanigans over the years. Kittehlicious for her midnight adventures across the world. Speedy Rope Guy for his medical play expertise, Alec and Chloe Bond for my Florida adventures. Lew Rubens for the inspiration and Peter Claver for joining in. Dr. Phil and his evening rigging in Paris, George and Anna and the whole gang at Northbound Leather. Maxine X and Scott for their undying support over the years. Archean for being scared of me from time to time and Mad Scientist for letting her. Gregg for being a demo bunny for people to torture over the years. Joey and Scott for helping with making my work look awesome online. Roy the lube boy and Kharma for both their support. Beret, Geoff and Garfield for the great discussions and encouragement of my photography. Dr. Carol Pukall at Queen's University. Joe for being my anchor in the US. Dart and his Domain, Cub Dan for being such a great bear, The Knoxville scene for being so incredibly welcoming, Come As You Are for encouraging my teaching career when I was starting out. Diana and the Shibaricon crew, Michael my Viennese hideaway, Stella Perversa and Dommy Darko, Byrd, Craiger, Sir Alex Dark and Johnny-Boy for being great bros. EMJ and the FetLife team. Tracy and Jeff Adams for being my token soulless Gingers. Don Sir for being such a great guy whom I never get to see enough of, Carrie Grey of Aslan Leather for her unmatched quality in leather toys, FetishCon in Tampa for being the craziest 4 days of my year as well as Cecil and Penguin at The Woodshed, FL. Most of all to you and everyone around the world who has ever come to my classes, been to the Morpheous Bondage Extravaganza during Nuit Blanche or complimented my work by picking up this book. Lastly, my family who will never read this book and don't understand my lifestyle but I love them regardless.

About the Author

Morpheous (Hons B.A., B.Ed) is a sex educator/author, photographer and magazine/kinkyTV/radio consultant based in Toronto, Canada. He is the author of two books: *How to Be Kinky: A Beginner's Guide to BDSM* (2008, Green Candy Press, San Francisco) and this one, *How to Be Kinkier: More Adventures in Adult Playtime* (2012, Green Candy Press, San Francisco). His work is archived at the Sexual Representation Collection at the Bonham Centre for Sexual Diversity Studies at the University of Toronto, the Leather Archives of Chicago and the National Archives of Canada. He travels and presents across the Americas and Europe doing outreach to both academic and kink aware safer sex organizations. He is also the host the world's largest single night public erotic Japanese rope bondage event during Nuit Blanche in Toronto, Canada.

Morpheous online: lordmorpheous.com
Email: LM@lordmorpheous.com